AF342603

The Intellectual Fraud of Meat-Eaters

Thomas Lepeltier

THE INTELLECTUAL FRAUD OF MEAT-EATERS

Max Milo

Max Milo Editions, Paris, 2023
www.maxmilo.com
ISBN : 978-2-315-01142-1

To the billions of animals
executed each year
in slaughterhouses.

Prologue. On the responsibility of intellectuals

Every day, millions of pigs, cows, rabbits, lambs and chickens are killed in French slaughterhouses. These animals end the short life they have spent, for most of them, without seeing the light of day, crammed into tiny cages or pens, in squalid barracks. When films about the daily life of these designated victims, or about the moment of their killing, are shown to the public, the images shock. Almost no one is indifferent to the fate of these battery hens; of these sows locked up for a large part of their lives in stalls where they literally cannot move forward, backward or turn around; of these piglets castrated without anaesthetic; of these chicks crushed alive or suffocated by the thousands in large plastic bags; of these cows whose legs are cut off while they are still conscious; of these calves torn from their mothers at birth; and so on. Faced with these horrors, everyone wants to shout, "Stop the slaughter!"

However, the massacre continues, day after day. Nearly 1 billion land animals are slaughtered each year in France (more than 60 billion worldwide). For fish, the number is much higher (more than 1,000 billion). Faced with this situation, a certain number of people decide to become vegans, i.e. to abstain from consuming any animal product (meat, fish, milk, eggs). This decision is, for these people, the only way to stop being complicit in this great massacre of animals. The approach is quite rational: since we can be in good health and eat very well without consuming animal products, why continue to make millions and millions of animals suffer and be slaughtered to feed ourselves? For a few years now, this approach has been supported by a growing number of associations, books, articles and documentaries that also denounce the consumption of animal flesh, eggs and milk for the simple reason that it always leads to the cruel exploitation of harmless animals, while not meeting any need.

This approach is eminently political. It is not a choice of diet to feel good about oneself. It is a desire to stop cruelly exploiting defenseless beings. It is accompanied by a very precise demand: the abolition of slaughterhouses, fishing and hunting. It is also not a new approach. For centuries, thinkers have argued that it is cruel to kill animals when it is not necessary and that we should therefore refrain from eating them.

Certainly, this precept has been very little followed. The consumption of meat, dairy products and eggs has never stopped. Nowadays, it is even growing rapidly in the world. Yet, at a time when the slaughter of animals has never been so great, the reasons for ending it have never been so clear.

Since the 1970s, a school of thought known as "animal ethics" has clarified the duties that we human animals have toward non-human animals. Even if there are still subjects of discussion on particular aspects of our relationship with animals, it is now established that we must not kill and cause suffering to an animal when it is not in its interest or when it does not respond to any necessity. This principle is already enshrined in the law: if you have fun crushing kittens in a blender, castrating a dog without anesthesia, locking a horse all its life in a tiny pen where no daylight penetrates, you will be prosecuted for animal abuse. You could be sentenced to two years in prison. So why do the authorities approve of crushing live male chicks, locking chickens in tiny cages all their lives, and slitting the throats of millions of rabbits, lambs, pigs and cows every year for no other reason than to flatter the taste buds of millions of consumers?

With the increasing diffusion of shocking images showing the reality of slaughterhouses and with the rise of an ethical reflection that puts forward solidly supported arguments in favor of veganism, one could have imagined a rapid development of this movement. However, even if the number of vegans is steadily increasing, they are still in the minority. Why is this so? One could easily blame the inertia of citizens who, even if they can no longer watch a cow being cut into pieces without shuddering, remain attached to their steak. Out of respect for their gastronomic tradition, out of weakness in front of the pleasures of the table, out of lack of reflection, they do not feel encouraged to make efforts to change their cooking recipes, even though their personal ethics force them to recognize that what happens in slaughterhouses is abominable. It would also be possible to blame those in the food industry who do everything they can to make consumers forget the suffering behind meat, milk and eggs. Another target could be the politicians who do not want to take on the very powerful economic sector organizing the production and distribution of these foods. However, if all these actors have undoubtedly their share of responsibility in the perpetuation of the great massacre of the innocent, they are not the only ones to blame.

The resistance to change is also supported by a large number of intellectuals (academics, experts, journalists) who regularly attack the animal cause (let us quote, without being exhaustive, Jean-Pierre Digard, Raphaël Enthoven, Luc Ferry, Élisabeth de Fontenay, Périco Légasse, Dominique Lestel, Jocelyne Porcher, Alain Prochiantz, Francis Wolff). Through books, articles and radio broadcasts, they criticize, denounce and mock animal rights activists. This is not insignificant. Because of their influence on society, they make a mark. Understand this. When a film is shot inside a slaughterhouse and broadcast in the media, most people are shocked. Then, confronted with the arguments of the vegans, they look for answers. What to think? What to do? What to eat? And yet, these intellectuals, even if they sometimes deplore the current situation of so-called "livestock", still come to legitimize their slaughter. Our fellow citizens conclude that the situation of these animals is sad, that it should be improved, but that it is not going to change overall: chickens, rabbits, cows, lambs and pigs are destined to end up on our plates.

This accusation is not exaggerated. The positions taken by these intellectuals are clearly aimed at criticizing or preventing, more or less explicitly, any attempt to put an end to the massacre of animals. Here are a few examples. In 2013, while reviewing for the weekly *Marianne* the book of the journalist Aymeric Caron in favor of vegetarianism, *No steak* (Fayard, 2013), the gastronome and also journalist Périco Légasse tries to refute the thesis of his colleague by asserting in a totally arbitrary way and in an intellectually very outdated manner that "eating steak is the proper thing for man"! It is true that the title of the article, "Touche pas à ma côte de boeuf!"[1], leaves no doubt as to the state of mind of its author. On the expert side, here is Jocelyne Porcher, a sociologist at INRA (Institut national de la recherche agronomique), known for her criticism of factory farming. In 2014, when asked by a magazine specializing in environmental issues whether we should stop eating meat, she replied, "[T]he first question to ask ourselves is not whether we should eat less meat, but how we can eat it better[2]." That says it all. Finally, one last example. The philosopher Élisabeth de Fontenay is the author of a reference book on the place of animals in philosophy, *Le Silence des bêtes. La philosophie à l'épreuve de l'animalité* (Fayard, 1998). This work earned her a lot of media attention as soon as it was a question of bringing

---

1. Périco LÉGASSE, "Touche pas à ma côte de boeuf!", *Marianne*, February 2, 2013.
2. Jocelyne PORCHER, "La question n'est pas de manger moins de viande, mais comment en manger mieux," *Terra Eco*, April 28, 2014 (available at http://www.terraeco.net).

Prologue. On the responsibility of intellectuals

an element of philosophical reflection on the condition of animals. But, in 2012, when a journalist from *Elle* magazine asked her if animals have the right to live, she expressed her doubts: "That's the big question. And I confess that I don't know how to answer it. Because, as soon as we are dealing with an animal raised for the purpose of feeding humans, it is contradictory to recognize its right to life. [...] If animals were no longer locked up in the appalling conditions of intensive breeding... it would be more bearable to take their lives[3]. In short, what bothers Fontenay most is not that animals are killed, but that they are killed in an industrial way. When the journalist seeks to know more and asks her if she eats meat, the philosopher replies, "Yes, but very little, and especially because I don't know how to cook!" Those who can cook will conclude that they can legitimately eat more meat than the great French philosopher of the animal cause.

These are only examples. But these few legitimations of the massacre of animals are symptomatic of a reactionary thinking that still dominates the French intellectual landscape. It is indeed displayed in numerous press articles, interviews, books and academic works. Each time, the basic principle of animal ethics that we should not kill and make suffer an animal that likes to enjoy life, just for our pleasure, is forgotten, misinterpreted, or criticized. Instead of reminding or defending this principle, one can read (or hear if the intervention is on the radio) statements that try to justify the consumption of animal products.

---

3. Elisabeth DE FONTENAY, "To be human, you have to love people and animals," *Elle*, November 30, 2012 (available at http://www.elle.fr).

What is their value? In our opinion, not much: they have no rational basis; they defy logic; they encourage cruelty. But they do support a society that, because it does not want to change its culinary habits, kills a huge number of animals unnecessarily. For this reason, it seems important to us to denounce them loud and clear; not for the pleasure of criticizing, but in the hope that this clarification will contribute to putting an end to the great butchery and serve to launch a constructive debate on the place of animals in society. That is why this book proposes to make a systematic and argued criticism of the ineptitudes of French "intellectuals" hostile to animal ethics. The aim is to denounce the imposture of carnivorous intellectuals, or, which amounts to the same thing, the intellectual imposture of carnivores[4].

---

4. Throughout this book, we defend the thesis that veganism is the only legitimate ethical position on food. But we sometimes use the word vegetarianism in order to echo the words of the intellectuals we comment on. For the same reason, we sometimes talk about veganism without addressing the issues of animal exploitation for non-food purposes. It goes without saying that the exploitation of animals for non-food purposes also poses serious ethical problems. However, in order not to lose focus, we do not address them.

The forgetfulness of ethics

"Science without conscience is the ruin of the soul". Unquestionably, nowadays, this saying of the humanist François Rabelais perfectly illustrates the attitude of a great number of nutritionists. Indeed, read their articles or books, listen to them on the radio or watch them on television: they give a thousand tips on how to eat well, but never say or write a word on ethics. Such negligence makes one shudder. Take Jean-Michel Lecerf, head of the "Nutrition" department at the Pasteur Institute in Lille. A recognized researcher, he is regularly invited in the media to give his opinion on food. In this role, he often advises the French to eat more rabbits[5]. The recommendation is perhaps not absurd when one is only interested in the relative qualities of the meats. However, for anyone with a modicum of conscience, it is more than disturbing.

---

5. For example, Jean-Michel LECERF, "There are no bad meats," *Le Figaro*, April 30, 2015 (available at http://sante.lefigaro.fr).

It is indeed important to know - and Lecerf should not ignore it - that rabbits are one of the most mistreated livestock in France. In fact, almost all of the rabbits that are consumed today (that is to say 99% of the 40 million rabbits slaughtered each year) come from industrial farms for which the regulations are very minimal. These millions of rabbits are crammed into wire cages located in buildings where, very often, daylight does not penetrate, where they can hardly move, where the wires on the floor of their cage hurt their legs and where about 20% of them die before slaughter. Yet Lecerf, without saying a word about where the rabbits come from, would like us to consume more of them! If his recommendation were followed, tomorrow it would not be 40 million rabbits that would be martyred, but 45, 50 or even more. One wonders if Lecerf has not lost his soul...

The excuse of human superiority

The neglect of ethics is not unique to nutritionists. Most defenders of the established order pay little attention to it. Let's take the example of Jean-Pierre Digard, an anthropologist, director of research at the CNRS (French National Centre for Scientific Research), and a specialist in the domestication of animals. His status and his speciality mean that he is often called upon to discuss the animal condition. For example, recently, he was invited to participate in a general public debate on the status of animals, organized by the AgroParisTech engineering school (October 2014). He was also featured in the magazine *Sciences Humaines* (June 2013) to present his ideas on society's relationship with animals[6]. Finally, in September 2016, he came to lend a hand to *Causeur* magazine for a dossier almost entirely charged against vegans[7]. He is thus a voice that is being heard in France.

However, in his interventions, Digard seeks above all to discredit animal defenders, going so far as to assert, in a 2012 article, that "animalist theses [...] show themselves to carry the seeds of a new obscurantism[8]"! The charge is strong. It must be said that Digard does not like to be concerned about the well-being of animals. In the *Sciences Humaines* article, we can read that he feels "more indignation at seeing dogs or horses treated like babies than at attending a bullfight[9]". In a 2009 article, he even regrets that INRA refers to animal welfare. He justifies himself by arguing that this concept of animal welfare "escapes any scientific definition and is therefore instrumentalized for extra-scientific purposes[10]". To speak of the "happiness" or "joie de vivre" of an animal would indeed, according to him, be too "tainted with anthropomorphism". However, it is enough to look at a dog going for a walk with its human companion to understand that it takes pleasure in running and frolicking. But, in order to look learned while denying the obvious, Digard speaks of risks of anthropomorphism!

---

6. Jean-Pierre DIGARD, "Résolument spéciste," *Sciences Humaines*, no. 249, June 2013.

7. *Id*, "Animalism is an antihumanism" [File: "Let's remain human, let's eat meat"], *Causeur*, No. 38, September 2016.

8. *Id*, "The Obscurantist Turn in Anthropology. From zoomania to Western animalism," *Man*, no. 203-204, 2012, p. 569.

9. *Id. at* 8-9, "Resolutely Speciesist," *op. cit.*

10. *Id*, "Reasons and Reasons. Des revendications animalitaires. Essai de lecture anthropologique et politique", *Pouvoirs*, n° 131, 2009, p. 103.

The other reason why he rejects the notion of animal welfare is that, in his opinion, the notion of health is sufficient: "If [animal welfare] corresponds to a good state of health of the animals, this notion is not new: breeders have been talking about 'healthy' animals for a very long time, and none of them (with the exception of a few incompetent professionals [...]) would be so inconsistent as to put on the market animals that are not 'healthy' and that they risk not being able to sell properly or at all! [p. 103]". In this mind-boggling passage, Digard almost assimilates livestock to objects whose "condition" should just be checked, a bit like a used car salesman checks their condition before putting them on the market. However, you don't need to be a livestock specialist to know that an animal that has lived a miserable life can still be edible and therefore marketable.

These cynical remarks by Digard are not a simple clumsiness. They serve to justify the exploitation of animals, the end of which he neither envisages nor wishes. To give himself the appearance of a "great sage," he presents it somewhat as a historical and societal necessity. He thus writes that the "reason" for opposing the claims of animal advocates "is a principle of reality [according to which] what does not go in the direction of human interests has no chance of being retained and of being sustained" [p. 105]. Two centuries earlier, one can imagine the Digard of the time asserting that there would be no point in seeking to put an end to Black slavery since white and slave-owning societies would always give priority to their interests!

Moreover, the similarities between Digard's thinking and that of the slaveholders do not end there. In the same way that the latter had a hierarchical vision of human "races", he believes that there is a "de facto superiority of the human species over other species". According to him, this is even a "fact" that has been scientifically established: "This superiority [of the human species], the result of an evolutionary process spread over some twenty-five million years, is not a creationist credo, but a scientific observation [p. 105]. Now the proposition is absurd: no modern scientific discourse resorts to this notion of superiority. There are certainly differences between species or between individuals. But a difference in this or that domain does not mean superiority in general.

Forgetting to think seriously about ethics, Digard also misunderstands the notion of antispeciesism that is often used to justify veganism. According to this notion, the species to which an individual belongs is not a relevant moral criterion for deciding how to treat that individual. It is the characteristics and interests of the individual that must be taken into account. One can of course be vegan for ethical reasons without being anti-speciesist. It is enough to consider that animals have a moral value. But an anti-speciesist must be vegan. Conversely, a speciesist justifies any kind of exploitation of animals by the simple fact that they are not human. He therefore discriminates arbitrarily. However, in his 2009 article, Digard considers that "anti-speciesism [is] led to indict and demonize humans, and thus to turn into an anti-human speciesism[11]." The claim is absurd because antispeciesism encourages opening the circle of morality to sentient animals, not excluding humans. Why then would he "demonize man[12]"? In reality, it is Digard who demonizes vegans with his misunderstandings. He illustrates this again by writing that they "claim, [...] in the name of anti-speciesism, equal treatment for animals and humans [p. 97]". This is not true. If anti-speciesist vegans believe that all sentient animals (human and non-human) should be treated equally, they believe that they should be treated according to their interests. In practical terms, this means that you don't give a pig the right to vote if it can't use it, but you do respect its interest in not being mistreated.

In his 2012 article, Digard also challenges the common analogy between speciesism (which he sometimes calls "especism") and racism. He believes that the two notions have "nothing comparable: while racism derives its monstrous character from the non-existence of races in humans, speciesism is absurd, since species do exist." To which he adds: "Anti-especiesism is therefore nothing more than a philosophical choice, which seeks to justify itself *a posteriori* by misunderstood or deliberately falsified scientific arguments: man and chimpanzee presented as almost similar

---

11. *Id. at* 104, "Reasons and Reasons...", *op. cit.*

12. Jean-Pierre Digard takes up this absurd idea in his more recent article in *Causeur* magazine (see *above*). By explicitly referring to it, the journalist Élizabeth Lévy can then write in the same issue of the magazine: "By dint of depriving ourselves of meat, we often end up eating humans. This is how anti-vegetarian cabals are built, with nonsense! See Élizabeth Lévy, "La ferme des animalistes", *Causeur, op. cit.* p. 51.

by virtue of their 98% common genes (forgetting the 2% of genes that are not common, the 'key genes' or 'switch genes', which make all the difference)[13]." Digard obviously wants to be clever with his science. Unfortunately for him, the reason why racism is monstrous is not the non-existence of races. Even if they did exist, racism would still be questionable insofar as it would consist in discriminating on the basis of an irrelevant criterion (race, precisely). In treating an individual, one must take into account his or her interests and individual characteristics, not his or her race. For example, if a person demonstrates that he or she has the ability to go to university, there is no reason to deny access, whether he or she is "white", "black" or "yellow". Anti-racism has nothing to do with the notion of race[14].

In the same way, antispeciesism is not concerned with the genetic proximity of certain animal species to the human species. Just because chimpanzees differ from humans in only 2% of their genes does not mean that antispeciesists do not want them to be hunted and eaten. It is simply because these primates have an interest in living and there are many other things we can eat. Certainly, the awareness of this genetic resemblance can make human beings aware of the fate of these great apes. But the consideration that is due to them is not based on this proximity. If tomorrow

---

13. Jean-Pierre DIGARD, "Le tournant obscurantiste en anthropologie...", *op. cit.*

14. A critique of this argument by Jean-Pierre Digard can also be found in David CHAUVET, "Les animaux, ces êtres de raison", in *La Raison des plus forts. La conscience déniée aux animaux*, edited by Pierre JOUVENTIN, David CHAUVET and Enrique UTRIA, Éditions Imho, 2010, p. 45-47.

The forgetfulness of ethics

extraterrestrials, whose biological structure would have almost nothing in common with that of human beings, were to arrive on Earth, would it not be monstrous to enslave them - if of course we had the possibility of doing so, despite their technological power? Conversely, wouldn't we find it abominable that these extraterrestrials use this pretext of a lack of genetic proximity to hunt humans like game? In short, like anti-racism, anti-speciesism is not based on biological similarities. As Digard rightly notes, it is above all "a philosophical choice". It is the choice of justice against those who, under the false pretext of human superiority, arrogate to themselves the right to make animals suffer and kill them for their own pleasure.

A contradiction of convenience

The misunderstandings about the notion of antispeciesism are not unique to Digard. Indeed, there is among some French intellectuals a kind of willingness not to understand. For example, in 2013, when a journalist from the *Nouvel Observateur* asked Élisabeth de Fontenay about the impressive current editorial activity (books, reviews, articles, films) around the animal question, the philosopher replied: "[It] is [...] a question that is a little too fashionable, and I sometimes see in this pervasive interest in animals a denial of history and a way of escaping politics[15]." This is surprising when one knows that this questioning of animals is eminently political.

---

15. Élisabeth DE FONTENAY and Akira MIZUBAYASHI, "What are we going to do with animals?", *Le Nouvel Observateur*, April 18, 2013 (available at http:// bibliobs.nouvelobs.com).

In any case, the journalist goes on to point out that, in her book *Le Silence des bêtes*, she emphasizes that most of the great Jewish writers and thinkers who experienced the world of the concentration camps and the death camps have written shocking things about animal suffering. Fontenay then argues that this analogy can only be made by writers: "[O]nly literature can dare analogies that one should not allow oneself as an ideologist or activist. [In my opinion, one should not write books about animals if one is not a writer. [...] The only way to safeguard the animal mystery is through literature. In other words, here is a philosopher who refrains from thinking about the analogy that could exist between the way animals are treated today and the way the Jews were exterminated. She prefers to leave this comparison to writers. Why does she do this? She does not say. An analogy can be more or less relevant, and therefore more or less useful for reflection. But, to know this, we must first think about it. By leaving its use to writers alone, Fontenay gives the impression that she is afraid of being committed by the conclusions she might draw from this analogy if it were relevant. It is, in a sense, a refusal to think.

This renunciation explains the misunderstandings that litter her words. For example, in 2013, in a book of interviews with journalist Karine Lou Matignon, she acknowledges that animals have rights[16]. At the same time, somewhat like Jean-Pierre Digard, she believes that "there is an animal hierarchy

---

16. Élisabeth DE FONTENAY, "Les animaux considérés," in Karine Lou MATIGNON (ed.), *Les animaux aussi ont des droits*, Éditions du Seuil, 2013, p. 118.

The forgetfulness of ethics

[p. 103]" or that there is "a scale of living beings, according to the nature or degree of their organization [p. 111]". She deduces that "it is necessary to consent to this hierarchy, without which [...] one exposes oneself to claim for the goose what one claims for the cow [p. 111]". This is a troubling statement. Why is it necessary to adopt a hierarchical vision in order not to claim the same thing for the goose and the cow? Is it not enough to recognize that these animals have different interests? Second, Fontenay never says what these rights are that animals should have. On the one hand, she sometimes asserts that the suffering of animals "should be systematically spared" [p. 115]. Yet, on the other hand, she continues to assert that they can be raised to be eaten, even though this cannot be done painlessly.

If Fontenay puzzles her readers, it is ultimately because she makes statements in which she seems ready to acknowledge that animals should not be killed, but at the same time she refuses to do so, although it is not clear why. Thus, when Matignon asks her if animals have "an interest in staying alive", Fontenay replies: "If, of course, they have an interest in staying alive, who could deny it? [Similarly, when she wonders "on what basis we grant ourselves the right to kill animals, to hunt, to fish," she replies that "there is no answer to that question [p. 152]. With such words, she could be welcomed by animal advocates. However, Fontenay does not cease to vilify them. She writes, for example, "Some promoters of 'animal personhood' [...] have [...] a heavy anti-democratic past [p. 101-102]." The accusation is gratuitous and unfounded. Who, among the great promoters of the "animal personality", would be antidemocratic? Her denigration is also evident when she says that she considers antispeciesism "politically dangerous" [p. 127]. Why is she so eager to denounce those who no longer want lambs to be slaughtered? The answer is quite simple: Fontenay does not seem to tolerate that these people emphasize the immorality of consuming animal products, since she herself "does not practice vegetarianism" [p. 155].

At least she acknowledges her contradiction: "[M]y distrust of ethical radicalism [that of vegans and vegetarians] does not prevent me from seeing a hideous contradiction ... between the careful care that daily provides for the needs of animals and the ultimate purpose of that care, namely slaughter [p. 154]." To perceive this contradiction is not unusual. Consumers of animal products often recognize that there is a contradiction between, on the one hand, their desire not to cause suffering and not to kill animals when it is not necessary, and, on the other hand, their failure to take this desire into account when they eat. But Fontenay's contradiction is much more serious. As a recognized philosopher, often invited to speak and much listened to, she legitimizes this contradiction. She suggests that we can live with it and that it is therefore not so bad to slaughter animals[17]. In short, she sets a very bad example

---

17. Note, with dismay, that the philosopher Vinciane Despret explicitly says that there is nothing wrong with living "in the discomfort" caused by this contradiction! Program *Les Chemins de la philosophie*: "Faut-il manger les animaux?", February 2, 2017, France Culture (accessible at https://www. franceculture.fr).

The forgetfulness of ethics

for all those who are troubled by this contradiction and are looking for a way out.

The call to cruelty

Sadly, the contribution of most of Élisabeth de Fontenay's colleagues is not of better quality. Take Francis Wolff, another well-known and respected philosopher, professor emeritus at the École normale supérieure on rue d'Ulm in Paris. His trademark, so to speak, consists in trying to redefine a proper of human beings, or what he calls "of man", forgetting that this term to qualify our species is somewhat sexist. Without much surprise, he puts forward the complexity of human intelligence. The approach is not absurd but fraught with pitfalls insofar as every species possesses characteristics that distinguish it, more or less clearly, from all others. To affirm that the human being is not an animal like the others is no better than to affirm that the lion is different from the other animals or that the aphid has a specificity in the animal kingdom. In any case, what would make this characteristic of the human being justify that he has the right to slaughter other animals for his pleasure?

For Wolff, the answer lies in a supposed refutation of the utilitarianism of Peter Singer, the author of *Animal Liberation* (1975) who played an important role in the development of animal ethics from the 1970s onwards. According to utilitarianism, an act is moral if, in a given situation, it contributes to increasing the amount of pleasure (or conversely to decreasing the amount of suffering) experienced by the people concerned, including animals. Singer notes that the suffering inflicted on animals to produce meat, eggs or milk cannot be balanced by the small fleeting pleasures that we derive from them, especially since these pleasures can easily be found on a vegan diet. He concludes that we should stop consuming animal products. This approach can of course be criticized. In fact, other leading figures in animal ethics, such as Tom Regan or Gary Francione, have explicitly rejected it. In their view, simply because most animals have interests (notably, an interest in not suffering and not being killed), they should not be treated as means to an end and, in this case, should not be treated as consumable goods. Despite their differences, these thinkers all come to the conclusion that veganism is a moral obligation. Under these conditions, it is difficult to understand how a refutation of Singer would be sufficient to justify, as Wolff thinks, the consumption of animal products[18]. In any case, Wolff's critique of utilitarianism falls flat.

For example, in a 2009 article, Wolff writes about fishing that people who, while aware that fish suffer when caught on a hook, continue to fish are "more rational" than those who would abstain from the hobby. The reason he gives is that fishermen "will ask themselves, on balance, why the fate

---

18. Certainly, Francis Wolff mentions Tom Regan and Gary Francione in his book *Notre humanité. D'Aristote aux neurosciences* (Fayard, 2010). The problem is that, unless we are mistaken, he only quotes the first once, without analyzing his arguments. As for the second, it is only discussed in relation to his idea of sterilizing pets and domestic animals, which, according to him, are otherwise always at risk of being exploited. But, without discussing Francione's arguments, Wolff simply says that this idea is an absurdity characteristic of antispeciesism. The process is all the more cavalier since this idea is far from being taken up by all antispeciesists.

The forgetfulness of ethics

of these pike, however unfortunate, should be more terrible than that of their fellow fish, eaten by larger fish [...]. After all, they will say to themselves, is it not the fate of small fish to be eaten by larger ones - or by the animal called man? And we cannot prove them wrong[19]". The argument is astonishing. Here is a professor of philosophy writing that we can have fun making animals suffer since they are likely to suffer in their natural environment anyway!

Continuing, Wolff argues that utilitarian "calculation" is of little help in ethical matters since one "compares the incomparable": how can one compare the suffering of the fish caught on the hook with that of the fisherman frustrated at no longer having the right to fish? Let us recognize that it is very difficult, if not impossible, to quantify precisely the sum of the sufferings and pleasures resulting from an action. That said, it would be bad faith to imply that the frustration of the fisherman could be equivalent, in terms of degrees of suffering, to the pain of the fish hanging on a hook and then dying on the bank of a river or the deck of a boat. Of course, there are more difficult situations to assess. As Wolff mentions: "[H]ow can one compare the pain of the starving wolf with that of the devoured lamb? [But this question has no bearing on the question of vegetarianism: whatever the answer to the wolf and lamb problem, it is obvious that fewer sentient beings will suffer by switching to a vegan diet. We are not wolves. So why continue to slaughter lambs for food?

---

19. Francis WOLFF, "Des conséquences juridiques et morales de l'inexistence de l'animal", *Pouvoirs*, n° 131, 2009, p. 144-145.

In his book *Our Humanity*, Wolff also claims to have detected a contradiction in antispeciesism: "Antispeciesism does not need to be refuted: it does that very well on its own because it necessarily contradicts its own principles." His idea is that if human beings "must be morally anti-speciesist, then they are *a fortiori* morally speciesist [since they] derive their norms and values from the characteristics of their humanity. Later, Wolff rephrases this idea in a slightly different way: "Antispeciesism is a pragmatic contradiction.... To say that only one species *should* be anti-speciesist is exactly the same as saying [...] only such and such a race (e.g., 'white') should not be racist - which is obviously absurd." To explain his point Wolff says: "If one should not discriminate on the basis of race, it is because one should treat all men equally. But that is where egalitarianism necessarily ends. For no kind of universalism can by hypothesis be extended to all animal species (what about rats? what about lice?), let alone to all living species (should we stop using antibiotics?). Beyond the limit of humanity, egalitarianism contradicts itself[20].

Unfortunately for Wolff, it is easy to see that such statements are smoke and mirrors, in the sense that they are disinformation and manipulation. First, where did he read that, according to antispeciesists, "only one species *should* be antispeciesist"? Antispeciesism is a principle of non-discrimination against species other than one's own. Ideally, all individuals of all species should adopt it. It is obvious that we are far from it. It is a pity. A lion will rather hunt a gazelle

---

20. *Id.* in *Our Humanity, op. cit.* section "Our Humanity in the Anti-Speciesist Mirror," Ch. 10 (electronic format accessed).

The forgetfulness of ethics

than another lion. But this does not make antispeciesism contradictory. It's a bit like Wolff saying that the requirement of goodness is absurd because only humans can make it a rule of life! As for his analogy with racism, it sheds no light. Even if there were only one group of humans (people, ethnic group, etc.) to refuse racism, there would be nothing absurd about this approach. It would even be more commendable if they were the only ones to pursue this ideal. Second, concerning egalitarianism, where did Wolff read that antispeciesists wanted to include bacteria and, in general, "all living species" in the circle of morality? They only include sentient beings. This egalitarianism consists only in saying that, just as one should not kill a human without a compelling reason, one should not kill, for example, a lamb without necessity. Where is the contradiction?

Not afraid of outrageousness, in 2012 Wolff accused animal defenders of being no better than those who plunge them into the hell of industry: "There are indeed two possible and opposite forms of barbarism in our treatment of animals: reducing them to things (which is what some forms of factory farming do) and elevating them to the status of persons (which is what animalism, the ideology I denounce, advocates). If you want to consider animals as people, you end up considering people as animals[21]. Of course, these words make no sense. Why should respecting the most fundamental interests of animals lead to mistreating human beings? To put it another way, how can one claim that the desire to keep

---

21. *Id*, "Man is not an animal like any other," *Studies*, No. 417, 2012, p. 494.

the lamb away from the butcher's knife "necessarily" (Wolff's word) leads to the desire to slit the throats of humans?

Certainly, Wolff sometimes recognizes the virtues of animal ethics. In his 2009 article, he writes: "If it is a matter of condemning cruelty, we should applaud it[22]." The problem is that he is blind to the cruelty inherent in animal exploitation. Indeed, according to him, to put an end to it, it would be enough to "improve the living conditions of cattle and pigs" [p. 146]. But there would be no question of "banning fishing and hunting, [and] imposing vegetarianism on everyone [p. 146]". Why not? Because if this were the case, we would see that "animalism, despite its generous claims, is not an extension of humanist values, it is their negation [p. 146]". Here again, the statement is surprising. If humanism is the ideology that believes that human beings have a "natural" supremacy over other animals and that they can exploit them as they please, then yes, anti-speciesism is anti-humanism. But if humanism is about extending the circle of morality to all beings capable of suffering and, in particular, to all vulnerable beings, then anti-speciesism is about "extending humanistic values. It is an inclusive humanism, not an exclusive one like Wolff's. It is a humanism that extends the emancipation struggles of slaves, women, colonized peoples and sexual minorities. Finally, it is a humanism that does not deceive its world by claiming that there is no cruelty in fishing, hunting and slaughterhouses. There is thus a real opposition of values between Wolff and the vegans. While

---

22. *Id. at* 146, "Legal Consequences...", *op. cit.*

the former is a champion of an ethic of gratuitous cruelty, the latter does not want to make an animal suffer and kill it when it is not necessary. The tragedy for the animals is that Wolff trained at the École Normale Supérieure a part of the "intellectual elite" of France…

A cruel arrogance

Among this elite, there is Raphaël Enthoven. A smooth talker, this very media-friendly philosopher has a column on Europe 1 where he analyzes "the morality of information." On July 1, 2016, here he is commenting on the event called "A Night Out in front of the slaughterhouses" and organized the day before by the association 269 Life - Animal Liberation[23]. This association, openly anti-speciesist, campaigns for the abolition of slaughterhouses. The event consisted of silent vigils during the whole night in front of about thirty slaughterhouses in order to draw attention to the cruel fate of animals. This action obviously displeased Enthoven, as this column shows, where he also tries to show a supposed contradiction of the antispeciesists. As farmers had also expressed their opposition to this event and affirmed that they loved their animals, the journalist who was answering the philosopher's question, and serving as a prop, began by remarking that one could find it contradictory to affirm that one loves animals while eating them. Enthoven replies: "Yes, perhaps, of course, but it is less contradictory than forbidding ourselves to eat them because we love them." This is a

23. Chronique *La Morale de l'info*: "Veganism is anthropocentrism," Europe 1, July 1st, 2016 (available at http://www.europe1.fr).

puzzling proposition since it seems to mean that you would be less in contradiction by devouring your beloved cat or dog than by lavishing it with caresses!

The journalist expressing his perplexity at such a statement, the philosopher clarifies his thoughts: "No animal whose digestive system allows it deprives itself of eating meat. However, by asking man [*sic*] to abstain from meat, the anti-meat "night owls" demand from man what animals are incapable of. In doing so, they establish a difference in nature between man and animal for the benefit of man. The result is a hyperspecism that tears man from nature and puts him on a pedestal by asking of him what he does not ask of any animal." Faced with this new paradox (antispeciesists would be hyperspeciesists!), the journalist reminds us that it was not hyperspeciesists who spent the night in front of slaughterhouses, but antispeciesists. Enthoven immediately replies: "That's what [these activists] call themselves on paper. [But this is not the case] since these [allegedly] anti-speciesist activists oppose speciesism, which places man at the center of nature, that is, above nature, with the value of empathy with animals. But empathy, which one is right to brandish, is like sympathy a properly human value [*sic*]. So that we are here in full contradiction. On the one hand, anti-speciesists celebrate the indifferentiation of man and animal [...]. But, on the other hand, they brandish values that only men can adopt by definition. This leads him to his conclusion: "The call for a modification [of] dietary behaviors [of human beings] is an admission that we continue to rank man above other species. The moral of the news is that anti-speciesism is anthropocentrism."

It must be said that the statement is confusing, to say the least. Indeed, why does Enthoven affirm that "anti-speciesists celebrate the indifferentiation of man and animal"? Where did he read that? It is absurd. Antispeciesists see that there are differences between human beings and other animals, just as there are differences between lions and other animals, and so on. Enthoven also goes astray when he thinks that asking human beings to adopt an ethical behavior that other animals would find difficult to follow is tantamount to placing the former at the top of the animal kingdom. How many times must we remind ourselves that taking into account a difference (in this case, the great capacity of humans to follow moral rules) is not the same as affirming superiority? Finally, if asking human beings to modify their behaviour was anthropocentrism, then everyone would be anthropocentrism, as this kind of request is omnipresent in society! In short, all of Enthoven's statements make no sense. We can only hope that he was not sincere when he said that devouring those we love is less contradictory than pampering them...

The apologists of murder

In 2012, Richard Millet, writer and editor at Gallimard, created a scandal. In an essay entitled *Langue fantôme. Essai sur la paupérisation de la littérature,* followed by *Éloge littéraire d'Anders Breivik* (Pierre-Guillaume de Roux Éditions, 2012) in which he criticizes, among other things, multiculturalism, he lends a "literary dimension" to the act of the killer who, on July 21, 2011, murdered 77 people and injured 151 in Norway. While condemning the acts of Anders Breivik, Millet asserts that this individual is "undoubtedly what Norway deserved and what awaits our societies that keep blinding themselves." He does not hesitate to see the Norwegian killer as "both executioner and victim". Faced with these comments to say the least disturbing, many people are outraged and consider that the writer can no longer occupy his duties as a publisher. In September 2012, Millet announced his "forced resignation" from the reading committee of Éditions Gallimard. Case more or less closed. But what never creates a scandal is the apology that Millet regularly makes for the killing of animals.

In several of his texts, Millet indeed expresses his deep contempt for vegans and haughtily defends meat consumption. For example, in 2013, he writes that animal defenders are "infantile adults[24]" who perceive "red meat lovers (but also foie gras lovers)" as "inhuman predators". This would be an error of appreciation on their part since, Millet tells us, in "the rural community where [he was] born, in the Limousin, a high place of breeding, [...] cruelty towards animals was not tolerated". However, the same Millet recalls, a few lines further on, that during the killing of the pig one could hear "the howling of the animal". He also evokes these "lambs [that] cried before the knife" and these "rabbits [that] shuddered" before their throats were cut. But Millet sees no cruelty in this. It is true that, for him, one measures "the degree of abasement of a society by the place it reserves for dogs, whose nuisance is considerable", and he is pleased that "the Stalinist ideologists" had "understood this" and "held trials of animals, elevated to the rank of "enemies of the people", then tortured and executed".

It is not so much the existence of abject remarks coming from a person accustomed to provocations that one must deplore here (there will always be despicable thinkers), as the publication by a major national weekly of this kind of position. Moreover, the same magazine does not hesitate to reinvite Millet to pour out his hateful prose against vegetarians as soon as it is a question of debating the fate of

---

24. Richard MILLET, "Éloge de la viande," *Le Point*, November 14, 2013 (available at http://www.lepoint.fr).

animals. Thus, in November 2015, after the publication of a WHO report stating that red meat is probably carcinogenic, he is invited to defend this type of food. He can then indulge, with impunity, in sexist remarks ("I have always doubted the sensual dispositions of a woman who does not eat red meat[25]") and insult vegetarians whose "snobbery" would consist in appealing to "sentimentality, a terrible form of mental cancer [p. 75]". In the end, hitting women, animals and vegetarians is more or less the same thing: it doesn't hurt... the one who hits!

Sad defense of cruelty

If so many intellectuals have difficulty perceiving the problem of animal husbandry and the consumption of animal products, it is largely because they think that there is no problem in killing an animal that has lived well. But few of them thematize and analyze this idea. This is not the case for Dominique Lestel. This philosopher, who teaches at the École Normale Supérieure, has made a name for himself in recent years by popularizing the idea that culture is not unique to humanity. Helping to reveal that the mental life of animals is richer than previously imagined, he has also questioned the practice of eating them. How can we allow ourselves to eat sentient beings that have a culture? Being a meat-eater himself, and probably not wanting to change his habit, he tried to show that vegetarians were wrong. His

---

25. *Id*, "For Red Meat," *Le Point*, November 5, 2015, p. 74.

The apologists of murder

reflections then led him to publish in 2011 a small pamphlet against vegetarianism, *Apologie du carnivore*[26].

Like many carnivorous intellectuals, Lestel believes that "factory farming is an ignominy [p. 121]". He has the merit of deducing that carnivores should reduce their consumption of meat. He even advocates eating meat only on special occasions: we should "make every meat meal a ceremony, even a commemoration, and limit our consumption of meat to these occasions, while accepting only meat from a well-treated animal [p. 124]. Unfortunately, as is often the case with this kind of statement, if not always, nothing is said about what is meant by a "well-treated animal. Nor does Lestel say anything about eggs and milk that are the result of cruel treatment of animals. That's a bit easy. In any case, in order to defend the right to kill an animal that is supposed to have been well treated, Lestel starts by denigrating vegetarians. He makes gratuitous accusations such as: "[T]he ethical vegetarian is a moral fundamentalist ready for anything [p. 10]", who "wants to [...] abolish man and animality [p. 15]".

Secondly, Lestel asserts that vegetarians adopt, without realizing it, the opposite attitude to that which they advocate. It would thus be the carnivores who would be anti-speciesist because "the fact of accepting to act like all predatory species constitutes the only true anti-speciesist position [p. 55]".

---

26. Dominique LESTEL, *Apologie du carnivore*, Fayard, 2011. For a scathing critique of this book, one can read with profit the article by Pierre SIGLER, "Apologie de la mauvaise foi. L'inconsistante *Apologie du carnivore* de Dominique Lestel ", *Cahiers Antispécistes*, n° 34, January 2012 (accessible on http://www.cahiers-antispecistes.org).

Conversely, the vegetarian "rehabilitates [...] the thesis of human exceptionalism by considering that he is the only carnivorous (or potentially carnivorous) animal that must place itself above its omnivorous animal condition by not assuming one of its central characteristics: the predation of other animals [p. 63]". Of course, such a discourse does not mean much. How can refusing to slaughter a lamb when other sources of food are available be a way of rehabilitating the thesis of human exceptionalism? Besides, if we followed Lestel's logic, we would be anti-speciesist every time we refused to walk naked in the street or to sniff our own behinds every time we met a member of our species. But the only thing Lestel wants to preserve from his "animal condition" is the consumption of meat. How strange...

In the same vein, Lestel accuses vegetarianism of being self-contradictory: "One of the major beliefs [of vegetarians] is that animals should not be made to suffer. But suffering can result from the suppression of a source of pleasure. Since the carnivore is an animal that takes great pleasure in eating meat, preventing it from doing so is tantamount to inflicting suffering on it. To impose an ethical vegetarian stance on it is therefore anti-vegetarian [p. 57]." The problem with this argument is that the presence of a victim is a fundamental element in judging an act, as we can easily realize by transposing Lestel's reasoning to rape. Let us imagine a situation in which one would question the appropriateness of prohibiting rape, given that those who are victims suffer. Lestel would only have to answer that such a law, by dissuading potential rapists from committing rape, would impose immense frustrations on them; consequently, by wanting to prevent people from suffering by being raped, this law would make others suffer; proud of himself, Lestel would conclude that prohibiting rape is not fair! No comment…

If Lestel ends up with such a confusing position, it is because he never distinguishes between a suffering that we would undergo in our interest and a deleterious suffering, which would harm our integrity. He abusively moves from a recognition of the real virtues of the former to an apology of suffering in general. This gives him the wrong impression of having shown the legitimacy of the suffering that is inflicted on livestock. It also explains his total misunderstanding of the position of vegans who, contrary to what he claims, do not reject all suffering, but simply condemn the fact that animals are made to suffer when it is neither necessary for us nor in their interest. Finally, this misunderstanding of what the vegan ethic is leads Lestel to make statements that are more than dubious, such as: "A man who would no longer inflict suffering on another living being would simply no longer be a man, or even an animal, because a fundamental principle of animality is precisely to suffer and to cause suffering [p. 86]." In addition to its meaninglessness (as if one would no longer be an animal or a human being by not causing suffering to another!), this statement has all the makings of a call to gratuitous violence.

Lestel recognizes that rehabilitating cruelty is not enough to justify eating meat. Indeed, even if in life one must be cruel, this does not imply that one must eat the victims of one's cruelty. As he considers "that the justifications usually given for the carnivorous diet are [...] rather inconsistent" [p. 93], he proposes to do better than other carnivores. But how to justify meat consumption from an ethical point of view? Let us recognize that Lestel sets the bar high. Indeed, he does not try to show that such consumption does not pose an ethical problem; he argues that "eating meat [...] is an ethical duty [p. 15]". As a result, it is the vegetarian who is no longer acting ethically.

To defend this thesis, Lestel begins by asserting that eating is a way of recognizing "the dependence in which each living being finds itself with respect to other living beings [p. 91]. At first sight, the argument is surprising since, if it is obvious that we depend on other living beings to live, nothing forces us to eat animals. We can eat plants. Lestel then tries to clarify his idea by writing that "one of the principles undoubtedly the most precious for the harmony of life on earth is [...] the principle of reciprocity and of generalized exchanges between living beings. The result is an infinite debt owed by man to animals and the ethical duty to commemorate it constantly [p. 94]". Where does this "infinite debt" and this "ethical duty to commemorate it" come from? Lestel does not tell us. But it is enough for him to add that eating meat is a way of commemorating this infinite debt for him to feel that he has demonstrated the ethical character of this consumption. Clearly, this is bordering on a petition of principle.

Lestel's second argument in support of his thesis that eating meat is an ethical duty is that it "constantly reminds us that we ourselves are animals made from the flesh of other animals and capable of feeding other animals. Eating the animal, in other words, is a positive way of affirming our fundamental animality [p. 114]. It is obvious that we are animals. But why would we need to eat animals to remind ourselves that we are animals too? Cows, goats and rabbits do not do this and remain animals nonetheless. There are a thousand other ways to affirm our animality: breathing, walking, eating vegetables, screaming, copulating, defecating, etc.

Lestel's latest imposture consists in inviting us to model ourselves on the Algonquin peoples of Canada. It is his little lesson in exotic wisdom, very "eco-new age", which can touch people because it surfs on the idea, quite widespread, that the native peoples lived in harmony with nature and respected the animals. There would be no harm in killing them if we did it like the Algonquins. However, what Lestel tells us about these indigenous nations is either not transposable to our situation or is ethically problematic. He begins by saying that, for the Algonquins, "[t]o kill an animal for food is acceptable, provided that the killing causes the least possible suffering to the animal [p. 102]. We are glad to hear this, but the information is not very precise, to say the least. Nowadays, any meat company could claim that it too ensures that animals suffer as little as possible, given the rates imposed by its shareholders. In order to evaluate this notion of minimal suffering, we must therefore know what necessity the Algonquins are subjected to. If they live in conditions that force them to eat meat, their concern to make the animals suffer as little as possible is respectable. If it is just because they like the taste of meat, or because they find it amusing, or because they associate it with a ritual of some kind, this requirement loses its meaning since, apart from any real necessity, causing the animals to suffer as little as possible would consist in not killing them (one always suffers when one has one's throat pierced).

This simple logic, however, is not to Lestel's taste. In his view, the question of whether meat is essential to the survival of the Algonquins is a question of "little relevance" (p. 104). He believes that meat should be consumed even when it is not necessary. As we have seen, we should do so to commemorate our dependence on the animal world. This is precisely what the Algonquians would do, integrating this consumption into "a system of gift and counter-gift, that is to say, a somewhat elaborate system of dependence" [p. 103]. The ethics of the carnivore would thus take "the form of an ethics of reciprocity [p. 105]". However, it is difficult to understand what reciprocity there is in the killing of an animal. We take its life, without giving it anything in return. But these considerations do not embarrass Lestel. Losing himself in a mystique of cruelty, he maintains that an animal that is killed makes "a gift of itself [p. 109]", that the killing of animals is a means of ensuring the harmony of the world and that "generalized predation constitutes one of the principles of this harmony [p. 105]". Sauve qui peut!

The deception of the gift of life

The idea that animals would give their lives when they are killed is not unique to Dominique Lestel. It is found among many intellectuals, notably Francis Wolff. But it is probably Jocelyne Porcher who has developed it the most. This sociologist at INRA focuses much of her thinking on denouncing factory farming. To emphasize her disapproval of the way this activity has turned out, she even withdraws the name of breeding and speaks of "animal production". On the other hand, traditional animal husbandry is favored by this sociologist. While "animal production" would be exclusively subjected to the economic imperative, this second type of breeding would comprise an affective dimension which would make all its value. Thus, as she wrote in an interview given to the newspaper *Le Monde* in August 2015, in traditional animal husbandry, it is "not a matter of appropriating sheep to take their wool [and] cows to take their milk." The primary motivation of this profession is relational: "[I]t's about living together, producing together and deriving a common benefit[27]." It is this bond that would be the foundation of animal husbandry. Killing animals would be just a necessity for it to be economically viable, but not its purpose.

One could wonder if this vision of breeding is not a little idealized. But let's move on. The fact remains that, even if a goal is laudable in itself, not all the means to achieve it are necessarily so. The question is always whether these killings are legitimate. It is here that Porcher resorts to the theory of gift, according to which every gift implies a counter-gift on the part of the one who was the recipient of the first gift. In this case, Porcher's thesis is that breeders have the right to

---

27. Jocelyne PORCHER, "L'industrie porcine us et abus des animaux sans contrepartie," *Le Monde* (suppl. "Culture & Idées"), August 29, 2015, p. 7.

take the lives of animals since they are the ones who gave them that life. In a 2002 article, she writes thus: "The original gift for many breeders is the gift of life. The breeder gives birth to his animals: on the one hand, because he decides on the reproduction [...]; on the other hand, because concretely, he is led, more or less according to the considered animal species, to give birth to the animal by participating in the birth[28]. In return, the animal that has received life from the breeder must offer him something: "The first of the counter-gifts of the domestic animal is to accept to live, and to live in the human *domus*, that is to say, in a world with human significance." It must also "accept the rules of the work, even anticipate the will or the desires of the breeder". All of this must be done in the mode of affectivity: "The breeder is emotionally involved with his animals and does not conceive of this impulse without reciprocity [p. 255]." Finally, Porcher believes that the animal gives its life to finish accomplishing its counter-gift. In the 2015 interview, she thus states: "Breeders work with animals but they know that at the end of this work, in the more or less long term, they will kill them. The death of the animals is the culmination of the work[29]." Ultimately, the animal would give back what the farmer has given it, which is life.

Needless to say, the whole point is tendentious, to say the least. First, the animal does not choose or accept to live with a farmer; it is forced to do so. The idea that

---

28. *Id*, "L'esprit du don : archaïsme ou modernité de l'élevage ?", *Revue du Mauss*, n° 20 (2), 2002, p. 254.
29. *Id. at* 7, "The Pork Industry Uses..." *op. cit.*

The apologists of murder

animals work is also far-fetched: how can we consider that cows from which we take their milk or that chickens from which we collect their eggs work? This notion of work is just a subterfuge to avoid acknowledging that animals are exploited. Then, it is obvious that animals do not give their lives. They would even do anything to avoid having their throats slit. But, in Porcher, the words take, give and steal are almost synonymous. In any case, the idea that breeders give animals their lives is absurd. In order to donate to a person, that person must already exist. You decide to give a gift to someone who, in some contexts, may feel obliged to give a counter-gift. But how can you give the gift of life when the recipient does not exist?

Finally, what obligation could this person to whom you have given life have towards you? Of course, a child is expected to show some respect to his parents. However, this is mainly because he or she would have received affection and a good education from them. Probably inspired by this filial duty, Porcher argues in the 2015 interview that animals must be provided with good living conditions in order for it to be legitimate to "take from them the most precious thing there is, which is their life [p. 7]." But the statement is delusional. Allowing a person to enjoy a certain quality of life never gives the right to kill him. Would you have the right to kill your offspring under the pretext that you gave birth to them and offered them the conditions for a happy childhood? One recoils in horror at such an idea. With animals, the situation is similar. From the moment they are born, they have interests that we must respect, as far as possible.

Probably feeling that she is pushing the logic of gift theory a bit, Porcher plays her last card by claiming that breeders allow animals to live better lives than they would have without them. Thus, in a 2011 book, *Living with Animals*, she writes that a breeder can legitimately kill an animal if the animal's life "has been ... better than it would have been outside of breeding[30]." In a 2007 article, she elaborated on this idea as follows: "Most domestic animals have prey status. [The shepherds did not enslave the sheep, they built an alliance capable of reassuring the animals and allowing them to live without the fear of the predator[31]. In short, for Porcher, the breeders are nice: they protect the livestock from predators. Isn't that a good enough reason to be a bit of a predator themselves?

Here again, this argument is abracadabra. Since when does protecting an animal give the right to slit its throat? In any case, to want to make believe that the breeders protect the preys from the predators is a pure imposture. Have you ever seen a farmer go into the countryside to try to protect animals? Of course not. He is not interested in the poor prey that is being eaten away from his barn. He is only interested in the animals he breeds. These animals were never threatened by predators before the farmer was in charge of them. To claim that the animals slaughtered by the farmer had a "better life than they would have had if they had not been raised" is therefore meaningless.

---

30. *Id, Living with Animals. Une utopie pour le xxie siècle*, Éditions La Découverte, 2011, p. 5.
31. *Id*, "Don't set the animals free!", *Revue du Mauss*, n° 29, 2007, p. 582.

In the end, Porcher's fundamental mistake is to want to preserve a way of life and a type of food at all costs, to the detriment of the animals' interests and logic. She loves animal husbandry, respects the breeders and takes great pleasure in eating meat[32]. As a result, to prevent this world from disappearing, she invents a theory in which any relationship with livestock is understood in terms of an alliance, a contract, an exchange, a debt to be repaid, etc. In a way, Porcher is reminiscent of those recalcitrant slavers who, faced with plans to abolish slavery, could not understand that they had no right to dispose of the lives of others. Like her today, they claimed that they took good care of their slaves, that they gave them work, that they offered them better living conditions than if they were left to their own devices, etc. They even claimed that the slaves were not the only ones who had the right to live. They even claimed that the slaves were grateful to them. There was a mutual respect between them. The idea of putting an end to this form of cohabitation therefore saddened them deeply. Everyone would lose, they said. Society as they had always known it would disappear. So they attacked the abolitionists with

---

32. While Jocelyne Porcher generally defends livestock farming to preserve the so-called good relationship between farmers and their animals, she recently admitted that she likes meat a lot: "I like pigs, but I also like Gascon or Limousin pork chops [...] The meat of a good breed of pig, well raised and killed with dignity [sic], is a treat without equal. [...] The meat of a good breed of pig, well raised and killed with dignity [*sic*], is a treat like no other." All of a sudden, his defense of animal husbandry seems a little less disinterested. This probably explains her departures from intellectual rigor! See Jocelyne PORCHER, "J'aime la compagnie des cochons... et la côte de porc gascon," *Causeur*, no. 38, September 2016, p. 67.

virulence, just as Porcher does constantly with those who want to abolish slaughterhouses and animal husbandry[33].

The tragedy is that this reactionary position of Porcher has a strong echo in society. Her status as an expert, a researcher at INRA, and her editorial prolixity, ensure her a great presence in the media. She is also the perfect alibi for the system. She vilifies the meat industry as much as she does animal rights activists. As a result, carnivores who, like almost everyone else, are indignant about the conditions in which animals live in this industry, but who do not want to question themselves, find in her their ideal spokesperson. It is very convenient since, by referring to an ethics of animal husbandry, it gives a good conscience to those who enjoy eating animal flesh. As we have seen, it does not even ask them to reduce their consumption of animal products (see the Prologue).

There is even a "school of thought" that is built on Porcher's work. If you are a young researcher, you can do a university thesis under her direction and pursue the type of thinking she developed. This is what Sébastien Mouret did, for example. After a lot of hard work, he defended his thesis in 2009 entitled *The moral meaning of the work relationship*

---

33. For another critique of Jocelyne Porcher's approach, see Enrique UTRIA, "La viande heureuse et les cervelles miséricordieuses," *in* Lucile DESBLACHE (ed.), *Souffrances animales et traditions humaines. Rompre le silence*, Éditions universitaires de Dijon, 2014. Article reprinted almost identically under the title "La "viande heureuse"", in *Cahiers antispécistes*, n° 38, 2016 (accessible at http://www.cahiers-antispecistes.org). See also this philosopher's "response" to Porcher's interview in *Le Monde*: Enrique UTRIA, "La viande heureuse," *Le Monde*, 1st September 2015.

between humans and farm animals: animal killings and subjective moral experiences of farmers and employees. The title alone raises questions: the researcher is interested in the killing of animals, but only through the subjective experience of farmers and employees. It is true that no one cares about the subjective experience of animals. In any case, this thesis received the *Le Monde* prize for research in the humanities and social sciences, presided over by the sociologist and philosopher Edgar Morin. It was then published under the title *Élever et tuer des animaux* (PUF, 2012). This shows the recognition that this approach enjoys. But what does this thesis say?

Mainly, the same verbiage on the notion of gift as in Porcher. For example, Mouret considers that the investment "of the breeders in the work rests on a *gift of good life* to their animals. This gift can be interpreted as a way of legitimizing the fact of killing them for food, and as a *gesture* of gratitude that aims to recognize [...] what they give to men: life[34]". In the same vein, he writes that, in a killing carried out by a breeder, "it is less a question of taking life than of receiving it [p. 71]". Or again, this killing "is less like a relationship of predation than a relationship based on a gift. The death given begins a "positive flow of life" [quote from Porcher] from farmed animals to humans [p. 71-72]". From this idea of gratitude in killing an animal that has lived well and from this mysticism of cruelty where a "positive flow of life [*sic*]" passes between the breeders and the animals, Mouret

---

34. Sébastien MOURET, *Élever et tuer des animaux*, PUF, 2012, p. 9.

shows that the former are aware of the moral problem of killing the latter. But he claims that one can kill and love animals and that, in order to continue to live with them, one must assume their killing. To cry!

However, Mouret is not at fault for anything. He has done a good job. His thesis is rich in field investigations, with farmers and slaughterhouse employees. He is just a victim of the system. To maintain the breeding, the French institution is ready to all intellectual acrobatics. The university approves. The daily newspaper *Le Monde* gives its support. The big names in research endorse. And everyone sits down to dinner for a leg of lamb with apples, a veal cutlet with cream or a rack of pan-fried piglet, that is to say, pieces of an animal killed very young, torn from its mother, probably mutilated to make the breeder's work easier or to modify the taste of its meat. Perhaps a breeder even loved it. But love has never prevented cruelty. Maybe he took good care of it. But there are executioners who take care of their victims. Certainly, he took it upon himself to put him to death. But an assumed crime remains a crime.

Rights Deniers

In January 2014, a young man, who called himself "Farid de la Morlette," was filmed violently throwing a small white and ginger cat into the air and then against a wall. He then posted his feats on a Facebook page. The images have raised a great wave of indignation on social networks to the point that the police have immediately initiated, successfully, an investigation to identify the author of this act of abuse. After a procedure of immediate appearance in front of the correctional court of Marseille, the young man was sentenced to one year in prison, in accordance with article 521-1 of the Penal Code which stipulates that any act of cruelty towards an animal can lead to a prison sentence. In the meantime, the little feline, named Oscar, had been found, concussed, with a broken paw. Justice was thus rendered.

However, on the day of Farid de la Morlette's trial, like every day of the year, in French farms and slaughterhouses, millions of animals were also sequestered, mutilated, crushed or slaughtered, without the justice system finding anything wrong with it. Why did Farid de la Morlette receive a prison sentence when, with few exceptions, breeders and professional "killers" are never bothered by the justice system? The answer is simple. In matters of animal protection, arbitrariness reigns supreme. While it is forbidden to mistreat an animal (article of the Penal Code mentioned above) and "without necessity [...] to voluntarily give death to a domestic or tame animal or one held in captivity" (article R. 655-1 of the Penal Code), the law is, so to speak, never applied when it comes to animals intended for food. As far as they are concerned, society acts as if they had no rights. Faced with this denial of justice, one might have expected French intellectuals to speak out. Isn't it their role to fight injustice with their pen? Unfortunately, many of them take up the cause of the torturers and deny that animals have rights.

The reference to human freedom

Let's not exaggerate: sometimes intellectuals have the idea of granting more rights to animals. For example, in October 2013, 24 of them signed a "Manifesto" aimed at changing the legal status of animals so that they are no longer considered in the Civil Code as "movable property[35]". According to these intellectuals, the capacity of animals "to feel pleasure and pain" should indeed confer on them "the most fundamental rights". They therefore ask that they be given their own legal category in the Civil Code between persons and property. The initiative is welcome. However, it is not without

---

35. Available on the 30 million friends Foundation website: http://www.30millionsdamis.fr.

ambiguity, since these intellectuals do not specify what they mean by "the most fundamental rights". One might naively think that a sentient being should be granted the right not to be killed unnecessarily. But many of the signatories of this manifesto are not vegans and, until proven otherwise, have no intention of stopping their bloody meals. They therefore give themselves a nice role by claiming to care about the sad fate of animals, without committing themselves to stop being complicit in their exploitation.

This ambiguity of the Manifesto appears explicitly in an interview given about it in April 2014 by one of its signatories, in this case Luc Ferry. After a discussion on the evolution of the animal question, the journalist asks this philosopher a fundamental question: "Can we give rights to all animals and remain carnivorous?" Ferry replies, "It is certainly not a question of making animals subjects of law, that would be perfectly ridiculous in my eyes, but simply of protecting them from forms of cruelty that continue to exist in a scandalous manner." How can Ferry, on the one hand, find it ridiculous to make animals "subjects of rights" (isn't this a way of granting them rights, as the Manifesto wants?) and, on the other hand, assert that animals must be protected against "forms of cruelty" (i.e., granting them rights, including the right not to be mistreated)? This would require some clarification. But Ferry prefers to leave it at that and brushes aside the journalist's question by asserting, "We can raise animals without making them suffer[36]." Not only does this answer leave out

---

36. Luc FERRY, "One can raise animals without making them suffer," *Le Point*, April 16, 2014 (available at http://www.lepoint.fr).

Rights Deniers

the problem of killing (isn't the right to life a fundamental right?), but it shows a complete lack of concern for the fate of livestock. Where did Ferry see that animals raised to be cut into pieces never had to suffer for their condition?

For those who know the writings of Luc Ferry, this incoherence is not very surprising. In 1992, this philosopher published *The New Ecological Order*[37]. In this work, which was very successful, Ferry reproaches anti-speciesists and ecologists, whom he lumps together, for turning their backs on humanism, and even for being the enemies of humanity. But to equate the former with the latter is already a sign of great confusion. Indeed, antispeciesists are not ecologists if ecology aims to preserve "nature", "ecosystems" or "biodiversity". Antispeciesists consider individuals, not species. They do not defend abstract entities, but rights holders. They do not seek to preserve "nature" as it is, but to diminish the cruelty of this world. Second, a strong idea of Ferry's throughout this book is that love for animals would undermine love for human beings. In other words, because of the respect we owe the latter, we should not love the former too much. As we have already seen, the idea is absurd. In any case, Ferry should have understood that contemporary antispeciesism does not stem from a love of animals (although it may sometimes be present): it is above all the expression of a desire for justice.

---

37. *Id.* in *Le Nouvel Ordre écologique*, Grasset, 1992. For a thorough critique of this book, we recommend Élisabeth HARDOUIN-FUGIER, Estiva REUS and David OLIVIER, *Luc Ferry ou le rétablissement de l'ordre*, Éditions Tahin Party, 2002. We take up some of their arguments.

Within this rather confused conceptual framework, Ferry attempts to show that animals should not be granted rights. The central element of his argument consists in affirming that humans would be beings of freedom whereas animals would be beings of nature. He thus writes that "the animal is programmed by a code called 'instinct'" and that it "cannot emancipate itself from the natural rule that governs its behavior", while the "situation of the human being is the opposite. It is par excellence indeterminacy [p. 46]". From this postulate, Ferry concludes that only beings of freedom can be subjects of law: it is "the faculty of tearing oneself away from interests (freedom) which defines dignity and makes the only human being a juridical person". To avoid ambiguity, he specifies that "reason, language or intelligence" are not "the qualities that qualify man as a moral being, [it is] freedom [p. 89]".

For all that, Ferry believes that we have indirect duties towards animals. Inspired by the philosopher Immanuel Kant, he argues that these duties arise from the fact that, unlike plants and *a fortiori* stones, animals, without being free, act as if they were free, with a view to an end. For this reason, there would be an analogy between humans and animals: "[T]he [animal] life, defined as 'the faculty of acting according to the representation of an end', [...] maintains a relationship of analogy with what constitutes us as humans." As a result, this animal life must be "the object of a certain respect, that which through animals we also show to ourselves [p. 124]". Unfortunately, Ferry does not specify where the respect that one owes to animals begins and ends. He only suggests that we should not kill them for fun [p. 124], without saying a word against most of the exploitative practices in our societies. The other problem with this conception of vicarious duties is that it does not involve any concern for the suffering of animals in itself; it just pins it on human behavior. This implies a total indifference to animal suffering when no human being is involved[38].

Ferry's first mistake is to start from a premise that does not hold water. How can he still advance the idea that animals are riveted to their instincts and that humans are beings of freedom? Is he so ignorant of ethological research that he does not realize that animal cultures also exist? Has he never noticed that a cat or a dog, in many situations, hesitates, thinks, makes tests, elaborates strategies, gives up projects? With a minimum of effort, he could also have noticed that any popular science magazine or any animal documentary shows that a large number of animals, especially vertebrates, are capable of learning, innovating, imitating, transmitting, etc. They can even perceive the consequences of their actions. They can even perceive the injustice of certain situations and act to remedy them, even though their action does not serve their direct interests.

---

38. Let us note that Luc Ferry has since felt the need to "go beyond Kant". In 2001, he writes thus: "In the eyes of Kant, a human being worthy of the name had to avoid mistreating animals, in which case their consideration was, according to him, more a matter of "respect for oneself" than for them. A fine idea, no doubt, but obviously insufficient: if there were not, in the animal itself and not only in us, something that arouses compassion, in what way could cruelty even appear as a lack of self-respect?" in Luc FERRY, "Le IIIe Reich et les animaux", *Le Point*, 25 May 2001. But this evolution of his thinking did not lead him to adopt a more coherent position, as we saw in the 2014 interview in *Le Point* magazine.

Ferry's second mistake is to reason in the wrong way. In fact, even if he were right in his assumption that animals are totally under the control of their instincts, it is difficult to see why this characteristic should prevent them from having rights. Let us take the case of a very young child. It is a being still subjected to its instincts, like breathing or sucking on its mother's breast, and which does not know how to move freely yet. Does this mean that he has no rights? No, of course not. At least he has the right not to be mistreated. Why should it not be the same for an animal that is also subject to its instincts? Freedom plays no role in this problem. To make it the necessary condition for an animal to have rights is completely arbitrary. In sum, Ferry uses a kind of rhetorical sleight of hand to legitimize the exploitation of animals: he advances the totally outdated conception that, unlike humans, animals are not free and arbitrarily postulates that only freedom makes the former moral beings, while refusing to apply this criterion to humans who are not endowed with this freedom, such as infants.

Let us recognize that Ferry's thinking is sometimes a little more complex, not to say convoluted. Just after having written that an animal "cannot emancipate itself from the natural rule that governs its behavior [p. 48]", he indeed advances that an animal can distance itself "from the commandments of nature [p. 48]". We should know! In any case, if he sometimes considers, after having said the opposite, that animals are beings that tear themselves away from their naturalness, he will not make them subjects of law. Why not? Because, in them, the distances "from the commands of nature are not transmitted *from one generation to the next* in order to weave a history [p. 48]". In other words, the great difference with humanity is that "the animal societies [...] do not have a history [p. 48]". Here again, one could discuss this alleged absence of historicity of animal societies. It is unlikely that they proceed by spontaneous generations. It is therefore necessary that their social behaviors evolve with time. But, even if his postulate made sense, Ferry should have understood that historicity is a notion that applies to a society or a group, and not to an individual. Therefore, it is absurd to make it a criterion of individual right. Otherwise, a wild child, cut off from any society and to whom the preceding generations would not have transmitted anything, could not be granted rights. In short, neither freedom nor historicity can be criteria for the attribution of rights. All that remains is to expect Ferry, who signed a Manifesto to confer on animals "the most fundamental rights", to follow through on his commitments, notably by stopping killing them (or having them killed by others)...

Rights and duties

On this question of animal rights, we also find Francis Wolff[39]. Without caricaturing too much, we could say that one of his strong ideas is that it is legitimate to slaughter animals for pleasure because these poor beasts are incapable of acting morally towards us. Thus, in 2012, after writing that

---

39. A critique of Francis Wolff's arguments on this issue of animal rights can also be found in Enrique UTRIA, "Happy Meat and Merciful Brains," *op. cit.* and "Happy Meat," *op. cit.* We are inspired by them.

"men are the only beings who act in the name of values and impose duties on themselves," Wolff argues that "the duties that men impose on themselves with respect to other men become rights for them insofar as they are reciprocal and universal[40]. Bad luck for animals: since they do not formulate duties towards us or towards each other, Wolff concludes that they cannot have rights. The big problem is that infants, some mentally handicapped and senile people, not to mention psychopaths, do not impose duties on each other either. Does this mean that they should be denied rights? This is probably not what Wolff wants. Yet to deny rights to animals, he would have to deny rights to humans who are incapable of acting on behalf of values, at least if he followed the logic of his argument. A society governed according to Wolff's principles would therefore be appalling[41].

Of course, Wolff does not explicitly say that one can enjoy making animals suffer, even if he is a defender of fishing, hunting and bullfighting[42] . The basenesses pass better when they are not confessed! Similarly, his insensitivity does not

---

40. Francis WOLFF, "L'homme n'est pas un animal comme les autres", *op. cit.* p. 493.

41. Francis Wolff responds to this "outliers" argument in His *Humanity, op. cit.* by writing that we must grant rights to outliers because "we recognize them as part of the human community [section "Our Political Humanity According to Animalism," Chapter 10]. This is to abandon the principle that only self-imposed beings have rights. But the new principle is no better. Making membership in the human community the condition for having rights is totally arbitrary. It amounts to saying that only humans have rights because only they are human! This is the same kind of arbitrariness that defines sexism and racism. Here, it is speciesism.

42. See for example Francis WOLFF, *50 raisons de défendre la corrida*, Fayard/ Mille et une nuits, 2010.

go so far as to make him think that it is okay to torture his dog. That is the limit he sets for himself. But how can we justify this difference in treatment between the pet and the bull in the ring, the rabbit in the rabbit warren or the fish in the river? Wolff simply considers that we have differential duties towards animals. Again in the same article, he writes thus: "[N]o one recognizes the same duties toward our pets, toward domestic animals, and toward wildlife: we are bound to pets by exchanges of affection, which we do not want to betray by abandoning them, for example [p. 493]." So far, the statement is reasonable. It amounts to a recognition that one has more duties to one's relatives than to strangers. From a legal point of view, you can be condemned if you do not provide sufficiently for your children when you have the means to do so, whereas you will be left alone if you do not help those who are dying of hunger at the other end of the world. However, this does not give you the right to have these children massacred. In other words, I agree with Wolff that one has more duties towards a pet than towards domestic and wild animals. But it is absurd to infer that this difference entitles us to turn the latter into fodder.

Concerning domestic animals, his position is no less problematic. Like Jocelyne Porcher, he evokes a supposed contract that would bind us to them. There is no need to repeat here how fanciful this idea is (see chap. 2). But let us recall that Wolff mocks his readers by writing that only "contemporary productivism, and its meat factories" would break this contract by not ensuring "respectful treatment of living conditions [p. 493]". Finally, on the subject of wild animals, Wolff writes that "the morality that binds us to wild species [...] is based on the respect of ecological balances and biodiversity [p. 493]". Here again, under the guise of a supposed beneficence - respect for ecological equilibrium and biodiversity - these words leave the door open to all kinds of abuse. They imply that you can slaughter wild animals if you think that this killing is beneficial to the preservation of the environment. You can even do it in abominable conditions since, in Wolff's morality, there is no respect for wild animals for their own sake; only the integrity of the environment should be taken into account.

It remains to be understood what these duties towards animals mean. Wolff insists on distinguishing them from rights. Yet, what is a duty towards a being that has no rights? If you have a duty not to abuse a child, is it not because of his right not to be abused? Let us imagine that he does not have this right and that you abuse him. Of course, you could be reproached for your behavior since you would not be acting according to your duty. But, since the child has no rights, no one could defend him in the name of his rights. This means that your duty would not really be a duty. It would be more of an advice or a wish, like "it is better not to abuse children". For it to be a real duty, it must be correlated with a right of the child. Unintentionally, Wolff thus attributes rights to animals, at least to domestic and companion animals.

Thinking a little too quickly that he has found a solid basis for his refusal to attribute rights to animals, Wolff is also mistaken in thinking that he has perceived the error of his opponents. He writes that "the notion of animal rights is contradictory [because] if we grant the wolf the right to live, we take it away from the lamb; and if we say that the lamb has rights, what do we do with the natural right of the wolf to feed? [p. 494] ". Let us recognize that the problem of the wolf and the lamb is not easy to solve. We are in a situation where there is a radical conflict of interests (the interest of the lamb and the wolf to live) and where there is no way to satisfy both interests at the same time. But this does not mean that the one who sees his interest violated had no interest. Thus the wolf and the lamb both have an interest in not dying: it is a right that we can recognize. The fact that the wolf does not know how to feed without devouring the lamb does not change this recognition. In a way, he has no choice. Therefore, he cannot be held morally responsible for his act. This sad situation does not imply that the lamb he killed had no right to live. He just didn't have a chance. An analogy can be made with the situation where a human being, because of his mental state, is declared not responsible for a crime he has committed. This legal decision does not imply that the victim had no rights. On the other hand, when a human kills a lamb for his own pleasure, or when he pays someone else to do so, he can be held morally responsible. He is violating the lamb's interest without compelling reason. In short, contrary to Wolff's claim, there is nothing contradictory about recognizing the rights of animals.

Moral relativism

In March 2016, during a program on France Culture, neurobiologist Alain Prochiantz also spoke out on the issue of animal rights[43]. When asked what he thinks about the animal cause, this professor at the Collège de France recognized that "the essential question, if we talk about animals, is that of suffering." However, after recalling that there is also "animal suffering" among humans, he adds that "from the moment we decide that we want to reduce animal suffering as much as possible, there are hierarchies in the types of concerns that we can have. The journalist then pointed out to him that this argument is a little specious because one can very well fight for peace in the world and be in favor of a respect for animals. This does not seem to be the opinion of Prochiantz who answers "no, because there is the question of law and the question of nature. [But it is humans who make the law". The journalist, having difficulty understanding this confused thought, retorts: why choose between the animal cause and the human cause? Prochiantz answers by saying that he "prefers the human cause[44]" and that the question of the right that is at issue here is important because "it is not a divine right, it is not a natural right, it is a right that is linked to this quite exceptional cortical development [of humans]". Then he adds: "Humans make law and this law is contingent, that is to say that, according to the times, according to the places, the law is not the same because they are not the same humans, because they are not the same historical periods." On the same register, a few minutes later, he

---

43. Program *L'Invité des Matins*: "Manger des animaux, est-ce inhumain?", France Culture, March 1st, 2016 (accessible at http://www.franceculture.fr).
44. Note that Alain Prochiantz has already developed this idea in his article "Mon frère n'est pas ce singe", *Critique*, n° 747-748, 2009. On the irrelevance of this position, see our chapter 7, section "Il y a plus important".

clarifies, "We can impose duties on ourselves towards animals; [but] this does not correspond to a right that they would have, otherwise we believe in natural law and personally I think that there is no natural right."

Do animals and humans have natural rights? That's a big question. So there is nothing shocking about not believing in natural law. To a certain extent, the claim that humans make law is not problematic either if we take it in the sense of positive law, i.e. the set of explicitly recorded legal rules. But can we adopt a relativistic position, as Prochiantz implicitly invites us to do? In ancient Rome, slavery was legal. Should we conclude from this that slaves were not victims of any injustice? No, of course not, because law is not limited to positive law or, to put it another way, because the legal is not always the just. On what then is this notion of right based from a moral point of view? To put it simply, let us say that law is based on interests. From the moment that an individual has interests, such as the right not to suffer, he has rights: the right not to be mistreated, the right not to be killed, etc. It is because slavery violates these interests or rights that it is condemnable, even if it was legal at certain times. It is for the same reason that the exploitation of animals should be prohibited.

But Prochiantz opposes this right of animals because, he says, "it is we humans who make law" thanks to our "quite exceptional cortical development". This position is ultimately very close to that of Francis Wolff and thus leads to the same unfortunate consequence that human beings incapable of formulating moral rules (infants, senile persons, and some handicapped persons) would not have rights. This is a pity, since Prochiantz himself had recognized that suffering is "the essential question, if we speak of animals". Why doesn't he see this as a source of their rights? Didn't he also mention the idea that we have duties towards animals? The philosopher Florence Burgat, present on the same program, even reminded him that recognizing that one has duties towards a person implies that he has rights. But Prochiantz, a poor student, proved unable to take this point into account in the rest of the discussion.

It must be said that he doesn't seem to care much about the idea of justice. In this program, he defends his position as a carnivore with an arrogance that leaves one speechless. His fault is not so much in expressing it ("personally, I'm for animal food; I like steak a lot") as in not admitting that it can be discussed. For example, when the journalist suggests that Prochiantz would tend to criticize vegetarians a bit easily, Prochiantz replies: "I am not criticizing anyone, everyone has the freedom to do what he wants according to his conscience or his self-imposed morals. [However, I am] always suspicious of those [vegetarians] who want to impose their own moral standards on others. Those people worry me. To which he adds: vegetarianism is "a matter of culture, that's it." For those who have not noticed, this is a mind-blowing statement. Explanation.

It is important to understand that morality or ethics is not a matter of taste. Each person is not free to choose his own moral criteria. These, once rationally defined, must be imposed on all members of a society, and beyond. For example, if some men find it perfectly normal to beat their wives, they must be called to order; they must even be condemned if they do so. There is no need to distrust people who, in this way, "want to impose their own moral standards on others". On the contrary, they should be congratulated. On the other hand, we should be concerned about those who, like Prochiantz, do not want moral values to be imposed. Their attitude is tantamount to leaving the door open to all kinds of violence against women, not to mention other misdeeds. Prochiantz' moral relativism is ultimately extremely dangerous.

In any case, as far as the vegans are concerned, we must put an end to the idea that they want to impose *their* moral standards. They simply ask their fellow citizens to be consistent with their own moral values. In fact, it is not only vegans who consider that one should not cause suffering and kill an animal when it is not necessary. Cruelty to animals is generally condemned in society, when of course citizens do not look the other way. This cruelty is even condemnable from a legal point of view. Farid de la Morlette was convicted of throwing a small cat against a wall just for fun. Prochiantz, on the other hand, can enjoy a steak from an animal that has been made to suffer and that has been cut down in its youth, just to satisfy his taste buds. He can thus put his whim before the life of an animal. It is this inconsistency that vegans condemn. They therefore demand that the right of animals not to be cut into pieces without compelling reason be finally recognized. Unfortunately, in order to prolong their little moments of plea-sure, many French intellectuals prefer to get lost in arguments rather than to recognize this elementary right...

The new Tartuffe

Many intellectuals are indignant about the miserable conditions in which livestock are kept today. But they rarely question the principle of breeding. The historian and editorialist Jacques Julliard is part of this trend. Certainly, he has made a few statements that might suggest that he condemns all forms of animal abuse. For example, in a November 2014 editorial published in *Marianne* magazine, he writes quite accurately that the "21st century will be the century of the animal cause. After so many other dominated creatures, the slaves, the proletarians, the colonized, the children, the women, everything indicates that the beasts are having their turn[45]". In a February 2013 editorial, he already wrote: "[T]he growing barbarity of modern man [...] has turned this planet, for all animals, wild or domestic, or farmed, into an immense slaughterhouse, a gigantic concentration camp, a kind of agri-food Nazism in the heart of the world that believes itself

---

45. Jacques JULLIARD, "Le sang des bêtes," *Marianne*, November 7-13, 2014, p. 6.

to be civilized[46]." Finally, he predicts that "the time is not far off when our descendants will blush at the treatment that this new century continues to inflict on the animal. They will not even understand that we have not been aware of our barbarity. In short, we want to applaud.

A closer reading of his editorials, however, reveals a somewhat ambiguous thinking. His criticism is only directed at meat production which is done in an industrial and religious way (halal or kosher). One can of course think that the small farmer treats his animals better than the industrialist. But both raise animals to kill them. Similarly, to condemn kosher or halal slaughter without criticizing stunned slaughter is to suggest that only the former is problematic. Certainly, for an animal, it is better to be stunned before having its throat slit. But, all things considered, it is better not to go to the slaughterhouse. So why doesn't Julliard, who sees the animal cause as an extension of the great struggles in defense of the oppressed, criticize this old unhealthy habit of killing animals to eat them? Why doesn't he take advantage of his editorials, published in a major magazine, to enjoin his readers to stop participating in the great massacre of the innocent?

If Julliard is content to condemn an abstraction ("industrial man") and a religious practice, it is probably so as not to make the readers of *Marianne* feel guilty for putting milk in their coffee every day, eating cakes made with eggs and enjoying a veal cutlet from time to time. In fact, it would

---

46. *Id*, "The Silence of the Beasts," *Marianne*, February 23-March 1, 2013, p. 4.

seem that Julliard does not envision an end to these culinary practices. In his November 2014 editorial, he finds nothing better to put an end to the horrors he denounces than to call for "great national conferences" where "conservative butchers" would be invited in order to elaborate "a minimal program aimed at public opinion and public authorities." If, in the society desired by Julliard, butchers are part of the solution, the blood of the innocent will always flow...

Cracking up at a chicken salad

Jacques Julliard embodies a certain form of self-righteousness that consists in condemning the cruelest aspects of breeding, without saying a word against its principle. The approach is very common. For example, in June 2015, Arno Klarsfeld called for the inclusion of animal rights in the Constitution[47]. This high-profile lawyer is also pleased that in India "the Delhi High Court has just taken tough measures against the bird trade." He seems to approve of the fact that the "Indian judge has made it clear that 'all birds have a fundamental right to fly in the sky and no human being is allowed to keep them in cages'. Yet, without realizing it, in the same interview, Klarsfeld tramples on the principles he has just defended.

Why introduce a right for animals into the Constitution? From what he has just said, one would have thought that Klarsfeld would want to recognize at least the right to live in freedom. Not at all. The interest of this recognition is simply

47. Arno KLARSFELD, "Plaidoirie pour le droit animal," *Paris Match*, June 13, 2015 (available at http://www.parismatch.com).

that it "would allow [...] the evolution of religious rites, halal or kosher". Apparently aware of the limits of his claim, Klarsfeld adds: "We are not all going to become vegetarians overnight, but the least of the gratitudes in killing animals is not to make them suffer." The statement seems reasonable. It expresses a sense of moderation and some would say a realistic recommendation regarding the current situation of animals: if we cannot make society vegan, let's not make the animals we kill suffer anymore. The proposal is problematic, however, for two reasons. First, to claim that one is grateful to an animal that one kills unnecessarily is meaningless. The least we can do is not to kill it. Moreover, the proposition implies that animals that go through conventional slaughter chains die without suffering! Who is Klarsfeld kidding?

The other problem with this justification is that it flouts any idea of justice. By stating that "we are not all going to become vegetarians overnight", Klarsfeld implies that in order to respect the rights of animals, we should stop eating them. At the same time, by asking only for "the evolution of religious rites, halal and kosher", he relativizes the urgency to stop killing them. It is as if he were saying that there is no urgency to prohibit murders since there will always be individuals who commit them and that we should be satisfied with repressing the most horrible ones! Some indulgent readers may say that Klarsfeld's proposal is just a way to proceed step by step towards a vegan society. But are we really moving in that direction by perpetuating the idea that there is no ethical problem with killing animals to eat them as long as we don't do it in a way that is too abominable?

As is often the case, this lack of consistency in the argument is explained by certain culinary habits. On this subject, Klarsfeld informs us that he is "almost a vegetarian". Here again, the implication is that he should become one. That's fine. Unfortunately, he admits that he "has a weakness for chicken salad". This is finally a lawyer who believes that "all birds have a fundamental right to fly in the sky", but who nevertheless likes to find some of them in salad! It is less the admission of a personal weakness that is serious. Nobody is perfect. The problem is that by acknowledging in a cheerful tone that he can "crack" in front of a piece of chicken, he implies to his readers that anyone can indulge in his little bloodthirsty whims. Hence the interest in not recognizing too many rights for animals, starting with the right not to be butchered. The animals will appreciate[48].

The carnivorous hummingbird

With Pierre Rabhi, animals are not much better off. Here is a farmer, author, philosopher and lecturer, who asks that we stop "making our planet paradise a hell of suffering and destruction". With this objective in mind, he "defends a society that is more respectful of people and the earth[49]". Such a philosophy could seem to be conducive to the respect

---

48. Some might be tempted to say that these remarks by Arno Klarsfeld were clumsy. Yet, in November 2015, he reaffirmed that stunning allows "animals [...] raised to end up on our plate an indispensable dignity"! How can we see this as a defense of animals? See Arno KLARSFELD, "Les oiseaux ont le droit constitutionnel de voler dans le ciel," *Libération*, November 16, 2015.
49. This is how he defines himself on his website http://www.pierrerabhi.org (accessed July 24, 2015).

of animals. Rabhi will often speak in sympathetic and moving terms of these beings with whom we cohabit the earth. For example, in a book published in 2012, *The Song of the Earth*, he deplores the fact that we "give ourselves the right to brutalize them, to make them suffer in a thousand and one ways. [He finds this cowardly because we are dealing with innocence. Faced with man, animals are persecuted innocents[50]". Further on, he recognizes that animals have rights, including the right to live: "I affirm that the creatures around us have as many rights as we do. [...] I invite human beings to stop being predators and to look at animals with gratitude for all that they give us."

Seeing him describe animals as "persecuted innocents", one might have expected Rabhi to champion veganism. Not so. Of course, with his credo as an ecologist, he is not going to start defending factory farming and slaughter. But, in remarks that are meant to be full of wisdom, he nevertheless denies the animals that we want to eat the right not to be killed: "I am not saying that all men must become vegetarians overnight, but I would like them, when they have to sacrifice an animal for food, to do as the Amerindians did, by showing their gratitude and avoiding any unnecessary suffering." Again, what gratitude do we show to an animal that is killed for culinary pleasure? None. Then, how can one affirm that one should not "impose unnecessary suffering on animals" and at the same time not ask one's contemporaries, who live in a society of abundance, to become vegans?

---

50. Pierre RABHI, *The Song of the Earth*, La Table ronde, 2012.

The key to this inconsistency is found in an interview Rabhi gave in February 2015. As is often the case, there is the refrain against factory farming, which is said to be "the heart of the problem" of our relationship with animals: "Concentration outside the soil, inadequate food, diseases, stress, etc.: this is not admissible. This is not acceptable[51]. Any justice-minded person is happy to discover this conviction. But disappointment is once again the order of the day. First, according to Rabhi, why is factory farming unacceptable? Is it not because the animals suffer? Not at all. It is simply because "proteins derived from animal suffering are necessarily harmful to us"! In other words, behind the fine words, Rabhi does not care about justice for animals; only the interests of humans count. He draws the conclusion that it is possible to continue to kill animals if they are not treated too badly: "So, to continue to eat meat, yes that is possible, depending on the needs of each person, but everything depends on the conditions of production."

Then, the other reason for disappointment is that, concerning the consumption of meat, eggs and milk, Rabhi will put forward the personal choice of each one: "It is up to each one to choose his food. I myself am not a vegetarian. [...] Falling into peremptory diets seems to me dangerous. It is important that each person listen to his or her own feelings. He who wrote that animals are "persecuted innocents", who have "as many rights as we do", here he is also asserting that we have the right to kill them if we have the desire or the

____

51. *Id*, "The basis of life is health, the basis of our health is food," *Kaizen*, February 16, 2015 (available at http://www.kaizen-magazine.com).

The new Tartuffe

feeling. As if veganism were a matter of personal choice! It is a question of justice. Eating meat, milk and eggs causes victims. But, to feel less guilty, Rabhi invents stories. For example, he maintains that he needs "animal proteins" and allows himself to say that "we all carry within us a heredity that is difficult to deny [and that, in his] case, it is the meaty diet of the desert peoples. Yet this is the same author who invites "human beings to stop being predators". How to find one's way through this muddle[52]?

The vegetarian friend of butchers

Just to further confuse those who have questions about the consumption of animal products, we can count on the journalist Franz-Olivier Giesbert. In 2014, on the occasion of the publication of his book *L'Animal est une personne*[53], he was invited on many television platforms. This book and these media interventions were an opportunity for him to come out as a vegetarian and declare his love for animals. Giesbert obviously loves animals. He was very close to them during his childhood in the countryside and keeps a great interest for these beings that he perceives as brothers and sisters. He takes advantage of this book and his media

---

52. Those who still have doubts about Pierre Rabhi's lack of consideration for animals can read with profit an interview he gave in October 2016. Referring to dietary restrictions, which he believes make people sad, he exclaims, "Eat a steak and be happy!" The joy of dining with friends and family is essential." See Pierre RABHI, "L'alimentation est devenue suspecte," *Le Figaro*, October 21, 2016 (available at http://www.lefigaro.fr).
53. Franz-Olivier GIESBERT, *The Animal is a Person. Pour nos sœurs et frères les bêtes*, Fayard, 2014.

interventions to denounce the current conditions of animal breeding and slaughter.

The problem is that Giesbert's position is not without ambiguity. First, if he defines himself as a vegetarian, it is in a rather flexible way. In his book, he writes thus: "[I] never eat tuna, a sophisticated animal whose flesh resembles ours, but I can't resist sardines, which, for all I know, aren't very smart [p. 35]." In other words, with Giesbert, woe to the simple-minded. In another text published the same year, he acknowledges that, in terms of vegetarianism, he "is not a purist": "If I never eat mammalian meat, I regularly allow myself exceptions for chickens[54]. Strange vegetarianism! Eat your brothers and sisters, chickens! Here again, it is not a question of throwing stones at all those who do not adopt an irreproachable behavior towards animals. The problem is that by using all his media power to claim loudly that animals are people who can be "regularly" eaten, Giesbert delivers a very ambiguous message to all his readers and listeners.

A second problem with Giesbert's posture is that it does not really contain any criticism of animal husbandry and slaughter. He is even happy with the current situation, when the job is well done. For example, in his book, recounting a visit to a slaughterhouse that is not overly subjected to industrial cadences, he declares himself satisfied: "After going from one station to another, from the actual killing to the weighing of the carcass, the truth obliges me to admit that I found nothing to complain about. There was a hospital

---

54. *Id. in* Franz-Olivier GIESBERT (ed.), *Manifeste pour les animaux, op. cit.* *at* 44.

The new Tartuffe

atmosphere, a mixture of rigor and respect [p. 131]." His reproaches are thus addressed only to the slaughter which takes place at industrial rates and especially according to the Jewish and Muslim rites. It would be enough for the government to impose that animals be killed without haste and with prior stunning for Giesbert to be happy.

This strange posture of Giesbert explains why, while presenting himself as a vegetarian, he declares his love for butchers, at least those who have "respect for the animals [*sic*], for the breeders, [and] for the environment[55]". So he invites Hugo Desnoyer, a butcher who, it seems, supplies the greatest tables in Paris, to contribute to a book "in the glory of animals [p. 113]", aptly entitled *Manifesto for Animals* (2014). The butcher in question can then describe how he ensures that the animals do not tense up when he kills them and how, as far as he is concerned, he likes to cut the meat delicately, out of respect. He also tells us why he started playing classical music to his animals before he slaughtered them: "[It] calmed them down[56]." Clearly, they must appreciate it. Who wouldn't?

Enough sarcasm. Giesbert can like butchers. That is his right. However, by calling his book *Manifesto for Animals*, when it should have been called *Manifesto for Good Meat*, he does not help to clarify the problem of the consumption of animal products. It is not impossible that, through its

---

55. *Id.* at p. 113, "Présentation de Hugo Desnoyer", in Franz-Olivier GIESBERT (ed.), *Manifeste pour les animaux, op. cit.*
56. Hugo Desnoyer, "Avec les bêtes...", in Franz-Olivier GIESBERT (ed.), *Manifeste pour les animaux, op. cit*, p. 119.

criticism of industrial or ritual slaughter, it has encouraged some readers to become vegetarians. At the same time, singing the praises of certain butchers is to imply that meat consumption is legitimate. Of course, on this subject, Giesbert is not the worst defender of the system. The problem is that by claiming to speak on behalf of animals, while praising those who slaughter them, he is like a traitor to their cause. He leaves a bitter taste in the mouth because those who really care about animals will always regret that he did not take advantage of his media fame to ask loudly and clearly that we stop slaughtering them.

The avoidance strategy

In September 2013, the novelist Isabelle Sorente published a novel that depicts without concession the squalid
living conditions in pig farms, both for the animals and for
the staff. The book is entitled *180 days* in reference to the very
short life span of these sensitive and intelligent mammals:
180 days living in a closed building, on a concrete or slatted
floor, without seeing the light of day, before being sent to
slaughter; in other words, 180 days of misery. In order to take
advantage of the fact that a well-known novelist has taken up
a subject that is too often hidden in society, Armand Chauvel,
who runs a blog devoted to veganism, invited Sorente to give
him an interview[57]. Going straight to the point, he asks the
novelist what she thinks about "vegetarianism as a response
to factory farming". Very surprisingly, Sorente replies,
"Factory farming is not a problem to be solved, a problem
that would involve a tailored solution, that would be far too

---

57. Isabelle SORENTE, "Novelist Isabelle Sorente demystifies vegetarianism,"
Vegeshopper, October 15, 2013 (available at http://www.vegeshopper.com).

rationalistic a way of looking at a life and death issue." She goes on to say that the way we choose to make millions of living beings live and die "can only be individual" and "that vegetarianism is not 'the solution'." It's really a shame! For once a well-known novelist talks about the abomination of factory farming, it is regrettable that she does not reflect on the main cause of this abomination.

Three years later, Sorente misses another opportunity to put her fame at the service of animals. This time, she was invited to participate in the program *Réplique* on France Culture[58]. She begins by saying that the visits she made to pig farms to write her novel did not lead her to become a vegetarian, despite their sordidness, because she wants to remain "integrated into this chain [...] of natural cruelty"! Why always this desire for cruelty? Then, after the philosopher Alain Finkielkraut, who hosts the program, has presented very positively the abracadabra theses of Jocelyne Porcher, Sorente follows him and argues that the latter has the merit to accept "the tragic destiny of the human". Finally, she pushes the nail in by affirming that she is opposed to substitute meats because, there again, it would be "a negation of the tragic destiny of the human being". It's like a dream! If there is a tragic destiny, it is above all that of the pigs that are born, live in deplorable conditions and have their throats slit on a chain. Once again, like so many other carnivores, Sorente ignores logic to avoid questioning himself.

---

58. Émission *Réplique*: "La littérature et la condition animale," France Culture, November 5, 2016 (available at https://www.franceculture.fr).

The art of evasion

This strategy of avoidance, finally quite common, sometimes borders on a form of cowardice. For example, in October 2015, on BFMTV, journalist Jean-Jacques Bourdin spoke with Brigitte Gothière, the spokesperson for the association L214, after the broadcasting of images taken in the slaughterhouse in Alès[59]. His interlocutor begins by explaining that these images are not specific to this slaughterhouse: they reflect a general situation. The killing of animals in slaughterhouses is never done without cruelty: the animals resist, are panicked, struggle, try to escape and suffer when they are stunned and killed. Bourdin acknowledges that the images of the slaughterhouse in Alès are "appalling" and that these poor slaughter conditions must be denounced. But he insists on asserting in a condescending tone his disagreement with the objective of the association to put an end to the consumption of meat. Without breaking down, his interlocutor then asks him if he considers that "hurting someone without necessity is fair?" Bourdin can only acknowledge that "it is unfair". Pushing his advantage, his interlocutor asks him if it is fair to kill animals that "are sentient beings; [that] want to live". But, this time, Bourdin refuses to answer. Distraught, caught in the trap of logic, he cuts short any discussion and moves on.

Where this lack of courage becomes pathetic is when, a few months later, Bourdin receives the Minister of Agriculture,

---

59. *Bourdin Direct* broadcast, BFMTV, October 15, 2015 (available at http://rmc.bfmtv.com).

Stéphane Le Foll[60]. The journalist asks him about a recent bill to ban the force-feeding of geese and ducks because of the cruelty of this practice. Not surprisingly, the Minister expressed his disagreement with the proposed law and argued that this practice is a tradition that must be preserved. He went on to say that of course "animal welfare must be respected" and maintained that he was committed to this. It is therefore necessary, according to him, "to stop these debates". Without batting an eyelid, Bourdin obeys and moves on to another subject. Strange. While he knows the method of making foie gras, how can he let the minister get away with it? How can he not laugh in his face when the latter claims that there can be a respect for animals in force-feeding? To let such an untruth pass without being contradicted does not honor the profession of journalist.

Let us note that, to cowardice, some prefer bad faith. On February 23, 2016, the association L214 broadcast images shot in secret in the small slaughterhouse of Le Vigan, in the Gard region, certified organic. This is the kind of slaughterhouse whose merits are praised by the supporters of "happy meat". Not being subjected to the high cadences of the industry, the animals are supposed to be killed with dignity. But, unluckily, the images broadcast are terrible. We see animals suspended by one leg regaining consciousness after being stunned and struggling as best they can; we see the staff violating the animals very harshly when they resist; and, to top it all off, we also see the staff having fun by giving them

---

60. *Bourdin Direct* broadcast, BFMTV, January 27, 2016 (available at http://rmc.bfmtv.com).

electric shocks. Once again, France is in turmoil, especially since it is no longer possible to incriminate the industry. All the media are talking about it. In the flood of comments, the philosopher Raphaël Enthoven decided to make it the subject of his daily column on Europe 1[61].

In this one, rather than talking about the images themselves, he prefers to focus on the way they are presented. As for the images of the slaughterhouse in Alès, the association L214 had them commented on by a "media" person. For Alès, it was the actress Hélène de Fougerolles; for Vigan, it was the singer Nili Hadida. However, at the beginning of his column, Enthoven reproaches these two people for concluding "the broadcasting of these appalling images with a profession of faith [in favor of vegetarianism]". The journalist who responds to Enthoven tells him that he does not see any problem with these statements and that these people have the right to be vegetarians. Enthoven replies, "Of course, but not to confuse the struggles." Then he immediately adds, "What is dishonest here is to implicitly equate eating meat with torturing animals [...], as if one were participating in the ignoble torture of a sheep that is ruthlessly thrown by one leg into a death box while eating lamb chops [...]. The problem is not that we eat meat. The problem is the way we kill animals. And that has nothing to do with it. To clarify his thoughts, Enthoven goes on to assert, first, "that there is no connection between torturing an animal and eating meat, otherwise all

---

61. Chronique *La Morale de l'info*: "Manger de la viande n'est pas un crime, et s'en abstenir n'est pas une vertu," Europe 1, February 24, 2016 (available at http://www.europe1.fr).

The avoidance strategy

predators would be torturers" and, second, that to be "vegetarian when you can eat meat is to challenge the animal in you and it is to put man on a pedestal."

On a superficial level, one could reproach Enthoven for drowning the fish. These are images that shock everyone and that he himself finds "appalling". Yet he prefers to attack the message that accompanies them, rather than address the problem they reveal. So it is not a column that is going to make his listeners think about what has shocked them. More fundamentally, Enthoven's comments reveal that he himself has not thought about this violence, because, although it is true that eating an animal is not, strictly speaking, torturing it, it still means supporting its killing. However much we may tell ourselves stories, killing animals is always violent for the simple reason that they do not willingly have their throats cut. Of course, slaughterhouse personnel do not always act with as much violence and sadism as at the slaughterhouse in Le Vigan. But all the testimonies confirm that this situation is not exceptional. This is understandable. The professional "killers" are not there to take care of the animals' well-being. They have to kill them, all day long. To be effective, they must necessarily desensitize themselves and stifle all feelings of compassion. Otherwise, they would drop the knives. As a result, acts of sadism occur regularly.

There remain the two "shock" arguments of Enthoven. As we have seen, the first one consists in saying that eating meat cannot be considered as torture, "otherwise all predators would be torturers". Indeed, predators are not torturers. The lion who eats the gazelle alive does not do it for fun or pleasure. It is a matter of life and death for him. But when Enthoven tastes a lamb chop, that is to say, the piece of a baby's corpse, he does it just for his own pleasure. He supports a system that tore this poor animal from its mother, mistreated it and cut its throat, just to make his meal more enjoyable. He thus encourages a cruelty that does not respond to any necessity. In this sense, Enthoven is complicit in a system that persecutes innocent beings.

Enthoven's second argument consists in saying that refusing to eat meat, when physiologically one can do so, "is to reject the animal in us". Obviously, as with Dominique Lestel, this is bordering on the delirious. There are many things that animals do, that human beings could do, but that they refrain from doing. For example, men could fight each other to get control of women and devour the children of their competitors. Yet they don't. Does this mean that they are rejecting the animal in them by not doing these things? Why then would abstaining from eating meat be tantamount to denying our animality? It is amazing to see a philosopher forget that ethics or morality consists in reflecting on the legitimacy of acts that one may commit.

Words and deeds

It is not very surprising to discover that many intellectuals refuse to assume their responsibilities. But with Michel Onfray one could hope for better. Successful author, very listened philosopher, his influence on the French society is undeniable. He is above all an intellectual who is not afraid to attack the dominant ideas and who shows a real concern for the sad condition of animals[62]. Moreover, he often repeats that one must judge a thinker by the way in which he puts in agreement his ideas with his way of living. The adequacy between work and life is, according to him, the mark of a great philosopher. So there was reason to rejoice when, in 2001, he acknowledged that "on paper, [he] fully adheres to the discourse that concludes the necessity of vegetarianism[63]". One might have expected him to declare himself a vegetarian and to urge his fellow citizens to become one. However, Onfray hastened to add: "in my life, I cannot do without fish, shellfish and meat in my cooking"! Once again, it is not so much personal weakness that is dismaying as seeing Onfray imply to his readers that one can very well not be a vegetarian even if one thinks that it is a necessity to be one!

Onfray is going to illustrate himself once again in this kind of discourse that recognizes the value of the arguments of vegans, but immediately scuttles the scope of this recognition by his refusal to take them into account on spurious pretexts. In March 2015, he published a collection of articles by thinkers committed to the animal cause in the collection he directs at Éditions Autrement: *Bêtes humaines? Pour une révolution végane*[64]. He deserves to be congratulated for having ensured the dissemination of these little known thoughts in the French intellectual landscape. Probably

---

62. See, for example, Michel ONFRAY, "L'animal, cette partie mémorielle de nous-mêmes," *Le Devoir*, November 14, 2012.
63. Michel Onfray, *Philosophie magazine*, n° 50, June 2001.
64. Méry PINQUE (ed.), *Bêtes humaines? Pour une révolution végane*, Éditions Autrement, 2015.

because he felt very interested in the subject, he wrote the preface to the book[65]. In it, after recalling some of the arguments in favor of veganism, he comes to the conclusion that vegans "are right [p. 10]. He seems to agree with them that it is not simply a question of improving the condition of livestock, as is often said, but of stopping their exploitation, because "to make a cow listen to a Mozart symphony before stunning it with a merlin and then bleeding it with a long knife is like putting flowers at the entrance to the Nazi camp [p. 10]. He even specifies that "the refusal of meat by the vegetarian who consumes dairy products is an insane ethical inconsistency [...]. To drink milk, to eat cheese, to eat dairy products, is to legitimize the murder of the young of the beast [p. 10]".

Unfortunately, after this encouraging start, Onfray pulls out of his hat three hackneyed arguments against veganism: the "carrot cry" argument, the burning house argument, and the disappearing human argument. Let's start with the first one. Onfray has learned that plants "communicate" with each other to defend themselves against aggressors. This reaction evokes in him a certain "vegetal intelligence [p. 12]" and an "authentic social intelligence [p. 13]". He even sees in it an indication that plants are sensitive. Onfray, proud of his discovery, thinks he can catch the vegans. They who say that one should not consume sentient beings, will they have to forbid themselves "to consume plants *as well*?" With this question, Onfray suggests that the position of vegans is

---

65. Michel ONFRAY, "Ce que tu fais au plus petit des periwinkles...", preface to the book by Méryl PINQUE (dir.), *Bêtes Humaines? Pour une révolution végane*, *op. cit.*

The avoidance strategy

not tenable. Anyone who seeks to become a vegan would either be suicidal (if he or she were consistent in not eating any sentient beings) or inconsistent (in eating some sentient beings, but not others).

The problem is that the characteristics of plants that Onfray evokes do not imply a capacity to suffer, which is a necessary condition for being the object of moral considerations. There are indeed many such vital processes that take place without consciousness, especially in animals (such as digestion, for example). It is also difficult to understand why, from an evolutionary point of view, plants would have developed this characteristic which would be of little use to them. When they are eaten, they can diffuse repellents automatically, but they do not have the possibility of evading those who chew them. An animal, on the other hand, not only has the ability to flee, but also has the means to choose its defense strategy, even if only by choosing the direction of its flight. Its reaction to an attack is therefore not predetermined like that of a plant. Moreover, in order to be able to speak of a sensitive being, there must be an individual capable of experiencing sensations of pleasure and pain. But plants do not have a central nervous system and each part is relatively autonomous with respect to the others. This characteristic, which makes cuttings possible, underlines the problematic character of any notion of individuality in plants. When a leaf is torn off a tree, which part would suffer? The leaf? The branch? The trunk? The roots? In short, it is difficult to see in a plant a sensitive individual. Besides, those who evoke a supposed sensitivity of plants to try to embarrass vegans do not really believe in it, otherwise they would have made the same objection to gardeners and soccer players who trample the grass a long time ago.

Onfray's second argument is that of the burning house. Here it is: "[I]f one day there were a fire and I had to [...] save either my neighbor's goldfish or my neighbor, it is without any problem of conscience that I would let the fish cook in its aquarium and that I would pull my neighbor out of the fire - even if she were my worst enemy [p. 13]." This kind of thought experiment is interesting for thinking about the respective moral values that we attribute to different types of living beings. Unfortunately Onfray does not understand that these reflections have no practical bearing on the question of veganism. In fact, whether or not it is necessary to save one's neighbor before one's goldfish does not make it legitimate, in any other situation, to kill the latter on a whim, in order to eat it for example. Why then would this supposed priority that we must give to human beings make it legitimate to consume cows, pigs and chickens? These animals are not in burning houses and, by eating them, we are not saving anyone.

Onfray's final argument is that "if [...] the universalization of the vegan maxim were to become effective, [the] thousands of species domesticated for millions of years by humans would become wild again; from that moment on, they would quickly do away with a human converted to the refusal to kill his nonhuman fellow man! [In other words, veganism risks leading to the disappearance of humanity. Clearly, Onfray forgets that, the day we stop eating cows, pigs and chickens, we will no longer make them reproduce at industrial rates.

The avoidance strategy

There is therefore no need to fear that they will overwhelm us. So when will Onfray start thinking[66]?

The disappearance of animals

Ironically, unlike Michel Onfray, most carnivorous intellectuals are afraid that, with the generalization of veganism, domestic animals will disappear from the face of the earth. Indeed, this is a scenario that even "vegetarian" Franz-Olivier Giesbert puts forward to justify his fear of vegetarianism becoming widespread. In a 2015 article, he writes that "there will always be steak lovers here on earth and [that] it would be wrong to deplore it: wouldn't a land without meat be a land without cows, and a land without cows, a land sad as death? Such is the great dilemma of vegetarians, who may ask themselves whether, by dint of their love for animals for slaughter, they will not make them disappear from the face of the planet[67].

---

66. Let us note that Michel Onfray himself recognizes that he does not think. Thus, in 2016, on France Culture, he allowed himself to say: "If I think, I become a vegetarian. And if I eat meat, it is because I have not thought. [...] Every time I think about the meat I eat, well, I think that the truth is on the side of the vegetarians and that even, in a way, the truth is on the side of the vegans." See the column *Le Monde selon Michel Onfray*: "Si je pense, je deviens végétarien," France Culture, April 2, 2016 (available at http://www.franceculture.fr).

67. Franz-Olivier Giesbert, "Pour l'animal, qui est une personne!", *Le Point*, November 5, 2015, p. 74. This desire that society not become vegan is moreover often found in this "friend" of animals. For example, in the same article, he also writes: "Let the meat-eaters reassure themselves: it is not a question of banning their favorite foods." Or, in his book *The Animal is a Person*, he writes that he intends to "encroach on no one's food freedom" but "simply demands respect for the animals to be eaten from birth to slaughter [p. 144]."

The form of regret expressed in these words is however misplaced. It is important to understand that the animals consumed have already almost disappeared from our countryside. In fact, in France, about 3 million animals (mainly chickens) are slaughtered every day in slaughterhouses. Over the year, that makes about 1 billion animals. For the most part, they are killed when they are less than a year old (calves are killed before 6 months; pigs are killed at 6 months; broilers are killed at 6 weeks). This rate of killing implies that, at any given time of the year, there are more than 100 million livestock on the French territory. Do you think that before being slaughtered they are peacefully frolicking in the fields and backyards? Of course not. Almost all of the animals consumed live in closed buildings, out of sight, in deplorable conditions. It is therefore always sinister to hear an intellectual put his aesthetic pleasure before the life of others and regret that the generalization of veganism will lead to the disappearance of cows, chickens and pigs[68].

Having said that, it is true that these animals only exist because we make them reproduce. If we stop eating them, there will no longer be any economic interest in bringing them into existence. However, the abolition of slaughterhouses does not imply their complete disappearance. In fact, there are several tens of millions of dogs and cats on the French

---

68. This indecency reaches new heights with the philosopher Alain Finkielkraut when he maintains that the disappearance of livestock would be a "nightmare". To avoid this aesthetic inconvenience, he therefore wishes that they continue to be born and slaughtered on a chain. *Répliques* program: "Faut-il politiser la cause animale?", February 4, 2017, France Culture (accessible at https://www.franceculture.fr).

territory. Why should domestic animals disappear completely if we stop butchering them? It is likely that chickens, pigs and cows will not become our new pets, at least not on the same scale. But there is nothing to prevent us from thinking that a small number of these animals could continue to live in the countryside, in a new form of relationship with human beings. For example, there are already shelters that welcome these animals without exploiting them. This type of experience could be developed. Rather than crying for the disappearance of concentration camps where millions of animals are kept, should we not rejoice in the fact that, thanks to the generalization of veganism, peaceful relations with domestic animals are being established?

THE CALL TO TRADITION

On Monday, November 9, 2015, members of the League for the Protection of Birds, including its president Allain Bougrain-Dubourg, were violently taken to task by residents of a village in the Landes region of France as they were conducting an operation against the poaching of finches, a protected species. The scene, both violent and bizarre, especially because one of the residents appeared in his underwear, armed with a shovel, was filmed by journalists present at the scene and then made the rounds of the media. The violence of the hunters was doubly blamed: first because it was exercised against a protected species, then because it was turned against those who came to oppose their misdeeds.

Taking advantage of the noise around this event, the humorist Guillaume Meurice made it the starting point of his column on France Inter two days later[69]. The principle of his "tickets" consists in asking simple questions to

---

69. Chronique *Le moment Meurice*: "Chasse au pinson," France Inter, November 11, 2015 (available at http://www.franceinter.fr).

various personalities and making his listeners smile, or even laugh, with the incongruous character of their answers. The one who is questioned is finally the turkey of the joke. That day, Meurice questions the president of the Landes Union of Traditional Hunting. He asks him: "Why does he hunt finches? The hunter replies, "Because we have always hunted finches in the Landes." Surprised by this laconic answer, Meurice reiterates his question by asking: "Is it just for that reason? The hunter confirms: "Yes. For what reason? We hunt because we hunt. Meurice, on the hilarious tone continues by saying with irony that, indeed, "we do not see why society should always evolve, otherwise you will see that one day we will give the right to vote to women.

With his column, Meurice has done an excellent job of making fun of the simple appeal to tradition to justify a cruel practice. Not that tradition has no value. It can reinforce our attachment to a practice that we otherwise find completely justified. But a practice, and a cruel one at that, must have other reasons than its antiquity to be defended. It is because he had not understood it that the president of the Landes Union of the traditional hunts was the laughing stock of the columnist of France Inter and of numerous listeners. Humor that played on the potentially dangerous character of this call to tradition. Indeed, what could not be justified by tradition? The male domination, as Meurice ironized? Or slavery, excision, torture, and so on? In short, it is clear that the appeal to tradition has no value as an argument.

The culinary tradition

Naively, one might have thought that this reference to tradition was no longer used by intellectuals to justify a practice. Unfortunately, this is not the case. Elisabeth de Fontenay is one of those who take pleasure in using it. Generally speaking, this philosopher does not like vegans. She says so and repeats it in almost all her interventions on the animal question. One of her complaints is that these animal advocates do not refer to tradition. For example, in the book of interviews with the journalist Karine Lou Matignon, she says: "What I reproach to the animalist radicalism, it is the non-taking into account of certain traditions immemorial [*sic*] anchored in the future of the men: that of the culinary tradition[70]." Despite the great philosopher of the animal cause, vegans make the consumption of animal products an ethical issue. Since their analyses have led them to conclude that eating animals is not moral, they have no reason to take into account the fact that this consumption is part of a culinary tradition. Would one criticize anti-slavery activists for not taking into account the slavery tradition of a particular country in their struggle for the abolition of slavery?

When a recognized philosopher appeals to tradition to justify the massacre of the innocent, the most serious thing is that this appeal is "intellectually" legitimized. Others can use it, even abuse it. The master of this is probably the journalist and gastronome Périco Légasse. In almost all his interventions on the animal question, he does not hesitate to

---

70. Élisabeth DE FONTENAY, "Les animaux considérés", *op. cit.*

oppose the merits of tradition, particularly French tradition, to ethical arguments. For example, in the fall of 2013, the association L214 had organized a campaign to broadcast videos showing the abominable treatment of ducks force-fed to obtain foie gras. As always, whenever images of factory farming or slaughterhouses are broadcast by the media, those who see them are shocked and the matter turns into a scandal. Precisely, to echo this, in November 2013, the radio station Europe 1 organized a debate between the aforementioned gastronome, defender of foie gras, and the spokesperson of the association L214, Brigitte Gothière[71].

The latter begins by reminding us how the force-feeding of ducks is similar to torture. The comment, in the form of a well-argued indictment, makes it difficult to defend foie gras. But, to preserve his little pleasures, the *Marianne* gastronome is not afraid of anything, not even to use big strings. First, with a good dose of bad faith, he denies that the images revealed by L214 are representative of force-feeding in general. He agrees that there are sometimes abuses, that the industrialization of the production poses a problem, but that it is possible to make foie gras without making animals suffer. He even goes so far as to say that "it is not because it is in a battery that it is badly done"; or he does not hesitate to say that "for foie gras to be good, the animal must be happy". Then, when he runs out of arguments, he repeats the appeal to tradition: "Nobody defends animal suffering [but] foie gras is a tradition [...] you don't take away the tradition of foie

___

71. *Europe midi - Votre Journal* program, Europe 1, November 29, 2013 (accessible at http://www.europe1.fr, starting at minute 53).

gras [...] we are not going to change, it is our culture [...] we will always continue to eat foie gras [...] we have a tradition, we have a civilization [...] you are not going to deprive us of foie gras [...]. We will continue to eat [...] foie gras because it is our way of life." Too bad Guillaume Meurice wasn't there to make us laugh by humorously pointing out the pitiful nature of these remarks.

Conviviality

The argument of tradition exists of course in less caricatural forms than "tradition for tradition's sake". One of its variants is the appeal to conviviality. This is more subtle because it seems easier to change tradition than to live in a world without conviviality. By saying that conviviality must be preserved, it is therefore possible to impose almost anything. At least that is what Elisabeth de Fontenay believes. For example, in a 2013 interview, she begins by saying, "I eat meat, quite a bit, but all the while considering that we should not eat it at all." So far, so good, since she implicitly acknowledges (through the use of her "it would have to be") that becoming a vegetarian is a moral obligation. It is afterwards that the subject becomes spoiled: "And, at the same time, it is a break that I do not want to make. I don't want to or can't take the step and break with the conviviality of a meal together[72]. The argument is surprising. Why can't a vegan meal be convivial?

---

72. Élisabeth DE FONTENAY and Akira MIZUBAYASHI, "Qu'allons-nous faire des animaux?

The call to tradition

One could see it as a clumsiness on the part of Fontenay. This is not the case: this is not her first time. Six months earlier, she had already made remarks that went in the same direction, except that they were even more confusing. As before, it started well, as she said, "[I]m not an activist but a philosopher who, I admit, has no philosophical reasons to continue eating meat." However, this good start did not prevent her from slipping up later: "[Eating meat] is for me, in reality, a matter of sociability. In my life, I have added enough marginalities [here Fontenay refers to her Jewish origins] not to add this one more. If I were a vegetarian, I would cut myself off from the community of human beings, at least from that of my close friends. I don't want to do that at all[73]. Now that's something to be afraid of!

Of course, it is not a matter of saying that it is always easy to become vegan in a society that consumes mass quantities of animal products. Sometimes you have to say no to dishes that are offered to you. This can make some friendly situations more complicated. But it is an exaggeration to say that becoming vegan is "breaking with the conviviality of the meal" or cutting yourself "out of the community of human beings". First, there are all the times you eat alone. There, you do not break with any conviviality because there is none. Then, there are all the times when you are the one who receives. There again, this does not pose any problem in terms of conviviality. So what is stopping Fontenay from inviting her family, friends and colleagues to eat vegan?

---

73. Élisabeth DE FONTENAY, "Pour être humain, il faut aimer les hommes et les animaux", *op. cit.*

She could make her guests discover that we can enjoy the pleasure of the table together without making animals suffer. Finally, there is the situation where you are invited. In the first case, you tell your host early on that you are vegan and he or she prepares a dish for you or for all the guests that meets your ethical requirements. The matter is settled. In the second case, you did not have the time to give notice. You refuse the dish or dishes that contain animal products, just to make your political opposition to the great massacre of the innocent clear, and your host improvises a substitute dish for you. Admittedly, this is a bit embarrassing since it complicates the preparations of the person who invites you. But, unless you have found someone particularly obtuse, there is no reason why the meal should not be a moment of conviviality. This refusal will even be a good pretext to expose to your table companions the ethical problem posed by the consumption of animal products. If you feel strongly about the subject, this is an opportunity not to be missed. What's more, this slight embarrassment pales in comparison to what's at stake. Beyond her grand declarations in favor of animals, isn't this finally an indication that Fontenay cares little for the poor animals that are being massacred on the assembly line?

As one might expect, Fontenay's status as a recognized philosopher has led to a number of emulators. Of course, it is impossible to know how many people are inspired by her excuse for not becoming vegan. But the damage seems significant. For example, in November 2014, the journalist Léa Salamé, on the much-watched show *On n'est pas couché*

The call to tradition

on France 2, explicitly referred to it[74]. The guest of the day is Franz-Olivier Giesbert who comes to talk about his book *L'Animal est une personne* (2014). On the set, after Giesbert criticizes the fact that, nowadays, animals are killed out of sight, in slaughterhouses where they are treated like things, Salamé begins by acknowledging that this is indeed a problem. Against this hypocrisy of society, she then declares that "we must assume that we kill them [animals]". The statement is astounding since assuming the killing of sentient beings who want to continue living does not make the act legitimate. It is not because a psychopath assumes his murders, without regrets and remorse, that they are legitimized. Salamé goes on to say that "the argument against vegetarianism [...] that touched her the most" was the one that came from "the mother of all [vegetarians], namely the precursor [*sic*], the tutelary figure of animal rights, [...] Élisabeth de Fontenay [*re-sic*]. She then quotes this philosopher who repeats that she is not a "vegetarian so as not to break with the tradition of conviviality". Aymeric Caron, also present on the set, intervened saying that he found "that this is a limit of her philosophical thought [that he] finds absolutely aberrant". Phew! But Giesbert and Salamé take him back, the former saying that he "understands very well the thought of Élisabeth de Fontenay [because he himself] is the same" and the latter arguing as if it were obvious that "there is a conviviality in sharing a roast beef". The problem is that, need we remind

---

74. *On n'est pas couché* show, France 2, October 11, 2014 (available at https://www.youtube.com).

him, to prepare this dish, it was necessary to slit the throat of an innocent man.

On the academic side, the damage caused by Fontenay seems no less great, when we see that Georges Chapouthier explicitly uses his argument of conviviality to "not cross the line. When it comes to animals, this philosopher and biologist is not just anyone. Emeritus research director at the CNRS, he is regularly invited on the radio or by magazines to give his opinion on various questions concerning animal ethics of which he appears, in France, as one of the great specialists. He is unquestionably in favor of greater protection for animals and is a vocal critic of the way our society views them. For example, in a radio broadcast in 2014, he said the following: "If man would look at the way he treats animals, he would withdraw covered in shame; it is abominable[75]." For all that, don't go asking him to stop eating them. Why not? Because he can't imagine "making the entire population vegetarian at once. Listening to these words, one has to be surprised. Who imagined such a thing? Animal rights activists do not believe in magic: they know that it is not with a wave of a magic wand that society will become vegetarian. There will necessarily be stages; the first being to become vegetarian oneself; the second, to incite one's fellow human beings to become vegetarian; the third, to ask for a law to abolish slaughterhouses; and so on. That the whole population cannot become vegetarian at once should not prevent Chapouthier from becoming one, if he

---

75. Program *Around the Question*: "Why is the animal a subject?", RFI, January 8, 2014 (accessible at http://www.rfi.fr).

really cared about the fate of animals. But no, that would be asking too much of him. He probably doesn't want to give up his little pleasures. One way of not admitting it, so as not to appear too shameless, is to resort explicitly to Fontenay's excuse. It is there that one measures his influence: "I am a little like Elisabeth de Fontenay, I think that to keep relationships with my fellow human beings, it is necessary to adapt to society as it is. [And] in our society, meat is friendly." Let's not return to the sad argument of conviviality. Let us note that Chapouthier adds to it a "we must adapt to society as it is". The proposal, given the context, is incomprehensible. Chapouthier has just recognized that our society treats animals in an abominable way. He should not, therefore, seek to adapt to this society; on the contrary, he should seek to transform it and no longer maintain what is abominable in this society. Instead, with the authority emanating from his position, Chapouthier suggests to his numerous listeners that there is no problem in devouring lambs, piglets or calves. How can we be surprised that the number of vegans is not increasing rapidly?

The pleasure

Other variations of the appeal to tradition include the reference to pleasure. As carnivores often say, meat or cheese "is too good!" So they don't see, they say, how they could do without it! Let's take the example of journalist Éric de La Chesnais, who deals with agricultural issues at Le *Figaro*. In the spring of 2015, in an article in this newspaper, he relates a poster campaign by the association L214 against animal milk[76]. This campaign consisted in putting up posters in the subway where it is reminded that, in order to obtain milk, calves must be taken away from their mothers a few hours after their birth. In a few lines, La Chesnais correctly reports on this campaign. Nothing to say. Even better: let's congratulate him for having reported on it, as our contemporaries are often unaware of the cruelty that hides behind dairy products. The problem is that, at the very last sentence of his article, he cannot help but scuttle his message by writing : "But it is also so good to eat a good fried rib steak ! Why this "belly cry", if not to tell his readers that, despite the cruelty involved in animal products, there is no question of doing without them, because "they are so good"?

The tragedy is that La Chesnais is not the only one to undermine any discourse on ethics in this way. For example, the same emphasis on pleasure is found in Boris Cyrulnik. This ethologist and psychiatrist is a successful author, seen by some as "our great national psychologist" and as someone who has "always been at the forefront of all the fights for the protection of animals[77]". It is true that he has long been interested in this field. For example, in 2013, in the book of interviews with Karine Lou Matignon, he wrote: "[T]he more we discover and accept the existence of a sophisticated mental world in animals [...], the more our empathy will compel us to stop doing anything with them. It is very annoying to discover

---

76. Éric DE LA CHESNAIS, "Une organisation de défense des animaux dénonce les veaux arrachés à leur mère," *Le Figaro*, May 29, 2015.
77. Franz-Olivier GIESBERT, "Présentation de Boris Cyrulnik", in Franz-Olivier GIESBERT (ed.), *Manifeste pour les animaux, op. cit*, p. 63.

The call to tradition

that the animal possesses, for example, emotions and an intimate world comparable to ours, because this limits our power over it, it becomes difficult to commit acts of violence on it[78]. To rebound on these remarks, the journalist asks him if it will not be increasingly difficult to consume them. Cyrulnik replies clearly: "That's right. The more we develop our empathy [...], the less we will be able to coerce them, torture them, kill them [p. 198]." Then he does not hesitate to emphasize the positive effect of this change: "[T]here would be fewer child martyrs if there were fewer tortured animals, fewer leaded wagons taking the victims of some dictatorship to their deaths if we had not become accustomed to vans where animals agonize without food and water on their way to the slaughterhouse [p. 222]." These are words that might make animal advocates happy. Unfortunately, they conceal a good dose of tartuffery.

In this interview, Cyrulnik makes a point of never taking a personal position on the consumption of animal products. When confronted with ethical questions, he has a very convenient way of placing himself in the future. He says that it is the coming discoveries of the rich cognitive and emotional capacities of animals that will force us to think about our consumption. As if we had no obligation today! Here again, the elusive character of this intellectual has a simple explanation. He reveals it, for example, in May 2016, during the program *Thé ou café*, on France 2. At one point, the journalist Catherine Ceylac echoed the slaughterhouse

---

78. Boris CYRULNIK, "Les animaux révélés", in Karine Lou MATIGNON (ed.), *Les Animaux aussi ont des droits, op. cit*, p. 197.

scandal of the winter of 2015-2016 and asked him if killing a pig, butchering a rabbit, or scalding a lobster were acts of cruelty for him. Cyrulnik then resorts to his usual strategy of answering using the future tense: "When we have understood that pigs are intelligent [...], it will be hard to [eat them]." After these fine words, which do not commit anyone today, the journalist asks him if he is a vegetarian or even a vegan. Cyrulnik finally lifts the mask and offers as his only answer, with the tone of one who licks his lips: "I love meat!" The debate is over. In short, pleasure justifies everything. You can claim that you have no right to kill animals and therefore, logically, to eat meat, but you can still do so in peace because you love the taste. What does it matter in the end that "leaded wagons" continue to bring "to death the victims of any dictatorship". When pleasure is the law, ethics go out the window.

For those who have not yet understood, justifying an action solely on the basis of the pleasure it brings is more than problematic. Imagine a rapist justifying his act by saying that "it's too good". He would be honest in the sense that it is indeed for the pleasure that this act is supposed to give him that he commits it. However, he would be despicable because he would not take into account the existence of his victim or victims. Some might reject this analogy. How can one compare a lover of cheese or "good meat" and a rapist who both say "it's too good"? However, to those who would be easily outraged, it should be remembered that comparison is not identification. No one is saying that eating a piece of cheese or "good meat" is the same as committing a rape. But the comparison is relevant because it reveals an analogy in the attitude of those who accept to make sensitive beings suffer in order to obtain small fleeting pleasures. In both cases, it is pitiful. Yet this is what Eric de La Chesnais, Boris Cyrulnik and so many other French intellectuals do.

The art of confusing

"Today more than ever, the animal is at the center of human concerns." This observation, relatively accurate, is what the journalist Théophane Le Méné made in *Le Figaro* in October 2014[79] . Unfortunately, it is not to rejoice. He sees it as a threat to human beings. According to him, there would thus be "a true and a false way of loving animals. The false one is exclusive, the true one inclusive". This little sentence is already clumsy, since it implies that we defend animals because we love them. But the animal cause is first and foremost a question of justice, as is the fight against torture, violence, unjustified discrimination, etc. You don't need to love children in particular to oppose their mistreatment. So there is no reason to think, as Le Méné then argues, that it is "difficult to celebrate the humanity of animals while consi-dering the respect due to humans. It is the opposite: to be indignant about the unjust fate of animals predisposes one

---

79. Théophane Le MÉNÉ, "Are Animals Like Men?", *Le Figaro*, October 20, 2014 (available at http://www.lefigaro.fr).

to be offended by the fate of human beings? But, without putting forward any argument, Le Méné repeats throughout the article that concern for the former would distract us from the latter.

For the misfortune of animals, this journalist did it again six months later, still in *Le Figaro*[80]. On the occasion of the "Day without Meat", he reproached vegans for adopting an "accusatory posture" that revealed "a crisis of the human being that they [vegans] fabricate under the guise of respect for the animal, through an attempt to erase the fundamental boundary that exists between man and beast. Here again, Le Méné continues his strategy of confusing the issue. Yes, vegans accuse their fellow citizens of still consuming animal products and thus supporting businesses that cause terrible suffering to animals. But where is the harm? No, they are not trying to erase the fundamental boundary (which one, by the way?) that exists between human beings and other animals. They merely point out that their differences do not allow the latter to be excluded from the circle of morality. Finally, how can Le Méné come to think that anti-speciesism "marks a real break with all civilization"? Is wanting to found a society on ideas of justice, altruism and compassion a break "with all civilization"? Sometimes you have to stop the delirium.

It must be admitted that, with Le Méné, the task will be difficult. After having criticized vegans, he now gives us the bottom of his thoughts. Appalling! According to him, "[t]o attribute to the animal any title to our respect is a mistake".

---

80. *Id*, "Journée sans viande: cessons d'être bêtes!", *Le Figaro*, March 19, 2015 (available at http://www.lefigaro.fr).

You read that right: no respect for animals! He claims that this does not imply that we can mistreat them. Referring to Thomas Aquinas and Immanuel Kant, he writes that we should not "mistreat the animal, not because the animal has a right to be respected, but because cruelty is inhuman. This rejection of abuse is of course welcome. Unfortunately, this concession is only abstract rhetoric, empty of meaning. How can we not see that behind a piece of meat or cheese there is abuse? This new confusion is explained by Le Méné's totally shameless character, as he reveals just afterwards. According to him, the animal does not have to be respected because, "if man is an end in itself, the animal is not. [...] We do not protect a species for an absolute reason but according to a calculation of contingent reasons: ecological balance, biological diversity, cultural heritage, etc." In other words, beyond the nice philosophical references to impress the reader, this conception amounts to saying that you can, without a qualm, imprison, crush, skin, trample, hit, force-feed, slaughter as many animals as you want. It is enough that you do it, for example, to preserve the gastronomic heritage!

More importantly

Unquestionably, the journalist Théophane Le Méné is rambling. This does not prevent him from being published in a major national newspaper. It is true that it is fashionable in France to make fun of animal rights activists. Rare are the journalists who, when they mention them or interview them, do not express a suspicion towards their approach. For example, in October 2014, the Buddhist Matthieu Ricard

The art of confusing

published *Plaidoyer pour les animaux* (Allary Éditions, 2014). A personality appreciated by the media, he is invited on numerous television and radio programs to present his work. A pedagogue, he patiently explains to the various journalists, who seem to know nothing about the subject, that his benevolence should be extended to animals. However, almost every time, the journalists who question him try to relativize the scope of his reflection by arguing that there are more important causes.

For example, it was Anne Sinclair on Europe 1 who asked him if he "doesn't feel like shouting louder [against the barbarities of the Islamic State in Syria] than he does about calves or cows and pigs[81]". It's Marc Voinchet on France Culture, when Ricard tells him that inside slaughterhouses "it's hell", who takes exception to these remarks because he finds "more urgent to be interested in the hell with Syrian children at the moment than in the hell with cows[82]". It is the novelist Éliette Abécassis on France 5 who, occupying for the occasion a role of journalist and while claiming to be a vegetarian, challenges him harshly by asking: "At a time when Yezidi women are being enslaved [*sic*], when hundreds of thousands of people are being killed in Syria, when the Kurds are going to be massacred, is it appropriate today to raise our voices in defense of animals or are we not here in

---

81. Program *L'interview d'Anne Sinclair*, Europe 1, October 4, 2014, (accessible at http://www.europe1.fr).
82. Program *Les matins*: "En attendant l'humanité bienveillante," France Culture, October 22, 2014 (accessible at http://www.franceculture.fr).

a form of barbarism [...] to take an interest in animals rather than men when men need to be taken care of[83]?" And so on.

There are several ways to respond to this type of argument. One can retort that compassion and a sense of justice are not divisible: one either has them or one does not. For example, Ricard likes to point out that his concern for animals does not prevent him from working for a number of charities that help human beings. He even argues that being sensitive to the suffering of animals - not only of one's dog or cat, but also of those with whom one has no particular relationship - would encourage one to be concerned about the suffering of humans, as many empirical studies seem to confirm. In turn, one can ask those who find it indecent to care about animals when so many human beings are suffering, what they do for them. It would be a safe bet that, in general, carnivores who are so easily outraged are doing nothing more than vegans who, as a matter of principle, refuse to allow sentient beings (human and non-human animals) to suffer unnecessarily. Independently of their personal case, they would have to explain in any case how the consumption of foie gras would be useful to the Yezidi women who suffer martyrdom or, conversely, how the refusal to sink one's teeth into a piece of chicken would prevent one from being interested in the ordeal of the Syrian children. Finally, against those who claim that "there are more important causes", one could also point out that they never accuse music lovers, soccer enthusiasts, card players, stamp collectors of not caring enough about

------

83. Program *Les Grandes questions*, France 5, October 16, 2014 (available on Matthieu Ricard's website, http://www.matthieuricard.org).

The art of confusing

human misery. Only those who care about animals, among other things, suffer from this accusation. This suggests that the carnivores who make this accusation are seeking, by this subterfuge, to evade their own responsibility for the cruel exploitation of animals.

It is not indecent to care about animals, otherwise caring about your garden would be. On the other hand, it is indecent not to care about them. To put cow's milk in your coffee is to maintain a professional activity where calves are torn from their mothers. Tasting cookies made with eggs is implicitly asking for hens to be hung by their legs and plunged into electrified water tanks before their throats are slit, all in a hurry. To swallow a slice of ham is to ask for knives to be shoved down the throats of sentient beings who value their lives. It is ironic that all these carnivorous intellectuals are indignant about those who find it unfair to kill lambs on a whim. They who claim to be in love with justice, approve the daily massacre of millions of innocent people, in France alone. Worse, they participate in it.

In our society, the omnipresence of this exploitation of animals even makes their defense acquire a special status. Indeed, in the current situation, almost all individuals who claim to want to help Syrian children encourage the slaughter of calves, chicks and piglets at every meal. Even if there were a hierarchy of causes to defend, why should we wait until a problem deemed more important is solved before we concern ourselves with problems deemed less important? Otherwise, there would be no need to take care of the unemployed, people with back problems or children with school problems because there is a war in Syria. But here, the situation is even more abracadabra. Indeed, those who believe that we should first care about Syrian children before taking care of livestock have, in their great majority, a share of responsibility in the misery of the latter. It is as if men beat their wives and are indignant that they are blamed for it because, according to them, the problem of beaten women is less serious than that of tortured children.

There is even an added indecency in scorning the claims of vegans. To put it quickly, one of the great differences with other causes is that the cruel exploitation of animals is legal. In our society, there are poor people, but the state does not voluntarily act to keep them poor; there are handicapped people, but no one wanted them to be handicapped; there is rape, but this crime is not allowed by law; there are battered women, but the perpetrators can go to jail; and so on. On the other hand, the French state organizes, supports and defends the killing of a billion land animals every year. The most dramatic thing is that almost all French people participate in this (while looking the other way, anyway). Such institutionalization of cruelty has few equivalents. How can one see the defense of animals as one looks at aid to the poor, to the handicapped, to rape victims or to battered women? The institutionalized nature of this cruelty turns the ideal of justice of the politicians and citizens of this country into a charade.

Finally, the disregard for the vegan cause is absurd on a practical level. In fact, as far as the Syrians are concerned, it is difficult to know how, on a personal level, one can help them to escape from their executioners. On the other hand, for the animals, it is very easy: you just have to stop eating them. So, to begin to reduce the misery of this world, there is not even a need to give money or time, let alone to go and fight: it is enough to abstain from consuming animal products. You don't have to get involved either; you just have to stop participating in the slaughter. This is why, while continuing to deal with the misery of the world in general, it is time for everyone to stop contributing to it as soon as possible. Unfortunately, the French do not like to be lectured.

No moral lessons

In 2010, the translation of Jonathan Safran Foer's book, *Faut-il manger les animaux?* (2009), was published in France. This book describes the appalling situation of animal farms and slaughterhouses in the United States. It does not leave you indifferent and, if you are not already, encourages you to become vegan. In that sense, it is a book that encourages you to question your morality. In January 2011, the journalist Aude Lancelin published an analysis in *Le Nouvel Observateur*. But, apparently embarrassed by this moralizing dimension, she tries to undermine the whole scope of the book[84].

Thus, although she is not obliged to do so, Lancelin cannot help but refer to the "goddess of reflection on animality in France, the philosopher Élisabeth de Fontenay". She then reminds us of the extent to which the latter has "always shown

---

84. Aude LANCELIN, "Ces bêtes qu'on abat...", *Le Nouvel Observateur*, January 13, 2011 (available at http://bibliobs.nouvelobs.com).

the greatest mistrust towards the champions of 'animal liberation', such as the Australian philosopher Peter Singer or Gary Francione". This stylistic device allows Lancelin to discredit the animal liberation movement. Is it not a sign that the animal liberation movement is problematic if the populist is suspicious of the thinkers who embody it? To get the message across, she adds without any justification that these "animalists [...] push to the point of absurdity the denunciation of the relationships of domination exercised by man over his furry and feathered companions". The reader who discovers these names with Lancelin's article cannot of course understand anything. He must imagine certain perversities or aberrations on their part. But what Singer and Francione, who by the way do not agree on many aspects of animal ethics, are simply saying is that one should not cut the throat of a lamb when it is not necessary. But Lancelin probably prefers to confuse the reader.

She continues with references to Dominique Lestel and Francis Wolff. By relying on the reflections of the former, she is able to suggest that there is legitimacy in the killing of animals: "[I]s it not possible to reconcile the idea of a respect due to animals, and even of an 'infinite debt' to them, to speak as Dominique Lestel does, with the acceptance of the carnivorous destiny of man?" As if the repetition of this hollow rhetoric (see chap. 2) were not enough, it is also necessary for Lancelin to insult Foer by calling him "a caricature of the young urban bobo, concerned with ethical irreproachability." About Wolff, she writes that his works have "shown with a rare intelligence" that "the long process of humanization through domestication, breeding and taming" have allowed "quite carnivorous civilizations" to establish a "relationship with animals that is not devoid of respect". In short, for Lancelin, if you no longer eat animals, it is because you are a young urban bobo who has not understood that human beings are carnivores and that we can respect animals whose throats we slit. So why bother?

Sadly, this article shows the harmful influence that some academics can have on the animal question (don't let them say that they have no responsibility for the abomination of slaughterhouses!). But he also expresses a surprising rejection, although very common in society, of any idea of morality and guilt. Indeed, Lancelin criticizes the book for containing "a few rhetorical sentences" and gives as an example the following sentence: "It is in our plates that one of the greatest chances of living according to our values - or betraying them - is found." This disapproval is surprising because there is nothing rhetorical about the phrase. It explicitly conveys a very important message. Eating is not ethically trivial. If you claim that you do not want to make an animal suffer just for your pleasure and that you consume animal products, you are betraying your values. If, on the other hand, you are vegan, it shows that you are at least trying to live by those values. Why then this negative judgment of Lancelin on this sentence?

It is not a question of style, since it takes up a reproach very often addressed to the vegans. In fact, almost every time there is a debate on the subject, they are accused of wanting to make their interlocutors feel guilty. In order for

The Intellectual Fraud of Meat-Eaters

their speeches to be listened to, they are told, they should not blame anyone and not address any reproach to anyone. This is a surprising complaint, since the message in favor of a plant-based diet cannot do without this moralizing dimension. It is an ethical issue, not a dietary one. If vegans invite their fellow citizens to become vegans too, it is because they reproach them for not being vegans. They want them to change. But these carnivores will not change their behavior if they are not pushed to do so, if they do not feel embarrassed to continue to consume animal products, that is, if they do not feel guilty. In fact, in a carnivorous society, one does not become vegan without effort. It is not difficult, but it does require the ability to say "no" and to think of strategies to avoid cruelty-based products. The determination to become vegan is proportional to the guilt one feels about eating off the backs of animals.

Of course, it is never pleasant to argue with someone who is trying to get us to adopt a more ethical lifestyle, especially if that person lacks subtlety. We don't like to have our immorality exposed. Ideally, the person we are talking to should never give us the impression that they are trying to make us feel guilty. We would then have the audacity to think that guilt would have developed spontaneously in us. But blaming someone for making us feel guilty about unethical behavior is a bit like blaming a messenger for bringing bad news. Yet this is the strategy chosen by many carnivores. Rather than questioning themselves, they prefer to blame vegans for using a moralistic tone in their comments or for wanting to make them feel guilty.

Even those who say they agree on the substance, but who are not vegans, often criticize them for being aggressive, sectarian, intolerant and for giving a bad image of their cause. They should be sympathetic. This is the great imperative of our time. This requirement is however completely misplaced. It is a bit like reproaching the persecuted for shouting too loudly when they protest against their misery, the raped women for being hysterical when they testify of their suffering, the despoiled for doing too much when they demand justice, etc. To reproach the victims, or those who speak in their name, for complaining in a way that would not be polite and respectful enough of the executioners is unfortunately part of a fear of questioning the established order. One criticizes on the form in order not to commit oneself on the substance. This is why Lancelin declares that some of Foer's sentences are rhetorical. She perceives too well the moralizing dimension. Since she feels caught in a fault and does not want to change her eating habits, she decides to attack on the form in order to confuse everyone. A sad expedient to avoid questioning the consumption of animal products...

Epilogue.
Tomorrow's debates

Most vegans today are not born vegans, that is, they were not born into a vegan family. They became vegans one day when they understood that the consumption of animal products posed an ethical problem and that it was easy to do without them. What would prevent French intellectuals, despite all their current resistance, from finally coming to the same conclusion tomorrow? This transition would even be very welcome. In fact, because of their own history, vegans are not going to blame them for being a bit "late to the party". In retrospect, they too invented excuses not to become vegans when they were first becoming aware of the problem. So they have very little grudge with the latecomers. If, tomorrow, Jean-Pierre Digard, Luc Ferry, Elisabeth de Fontenay, Franz-Olivier Giesbert, Périco Légasse, Dominique Lestel, Michel Onfray, Jocelyne Porcher, Pierre Rabhi, Francis Wolff and so many others recognize that it is necessary to put an end to these centers of extermination that are the slaughterhouses,

123

they will be welcomed with open arms by the vegans. All together, they will be able to share a great moment of conviviality around a good meal containing no animal products, happy to finally be able to join forces to shake up a French population still locked into its traditions.

Abolition on the move

There are many reasons to hope that this transition will take place in the near future. First of all, the strength of the arguments in favor of veganism has never been so convincing. Intellectuals should therefore not be able to remain insensitive to it for much longer. Secondly, the animal cause touches new people every day. Strong ideas are contagious and influence even those who protect themselves from them. One of the most beautiful manifestations of this awakening of consciences comes from certain breeders. For years, they led thousands of animals to the slaughterhouse. It was their job. They loved it, as they loved the animals they were taking care of. Then, one day, a cog in this beautiful routine of life and death broke. Sometimes it was the look of an animal getting into the truck that troubled them, as if it wanted to tell them something. But often there was no particular reason, just the accumulation of animals with broken destinies that began to weigh on them. Then a discomfort began to arise and gave rise to a simple question: why live off the death of others when it is not necessary? Unable to answer this question, their work became more and more difficult to the point that they decided to stop it and, feeling the need to follow the logic of their new way of thinking to the end, they became vegans. Some even became activists for the cause[85].

If breeders can become vegans, why can't carnivorous intellectuals become vegans too? Until proven otherwise, they are no more stupid than these breeders and, as they say, only the stupid don't change their minds. Tomorrow, as far as animals are concerned, everything can change in society. Jean-Pierre Digard, Luc Ferry and Élisabeth de Fontenay will write articles and books to show that a modern society must break with the carnivorous tradition. Périco Légasse will invite the readers of *Marianne to* stop consuming products obtained through the cruel exploitation of animals. Dominique Lestel will write a book of anthropology in which he will show that human society progresses morally when it seeks to reduce the cruelty of this world. Michel Onfray will finally bring his actions in line with his thoughts and will prohibit, within his "Université Populaire du goût", any product of animal origin. Jocelyne Porcher will spread around her the good news that one can love animals without cutting their throats. Franz-Olivier Giesbert will whisper in the ears of the politicians and the big bosses of the press that the exploitation of animals must be banned from society. Pierre Rabhi will preach to all the followers of moderation that consuming milk, eggs and meat is worse than encouraging industrial agriculture. As for Francis Wolff, he will meet with his fellow philosophers to show them that it is

---

85. There are multiple accounts of this type of "conversion". See, for example, Dominic HOFBAUER, "When Love is (Really) in the Meadow," *HuffPost C'est la vie*, November 10, 2014 (available at http://www.huffingtonpost.fr).

necessary to put an end to the great massacre of innocents. With this awakening of the intellectuals, public opinion will massively turn towards veganism. Then, forced to adapt to the times, the parliamentarians will end up voting for the abolition of slaughterhouses, hunting and fishing. A page of history will be turned...

At the same time, it will of course be necessary to organize the conversion of an important sector of the economy. People, especially farmers, fishermen and those who work in slaughterhouses, will have to change jobs. For the same reason, entire sections of the food industry will have to be abandoned. Agriculture, which depends in part on animal products, will also have to be reformed. Trade, whether it be small or large-scale distribution, or even international trade, will also be affected, as will many activities that revolve around the exploitation of animals. In short, this abolition of slaughterhouses, fishing and hunting will be accompanied by a great transformation of society. Of course, it is important that there are no losers. The fault is indeed collective. It is not the breeders or the slaughterhouse workers who are responsible for the misery of the animals. The whole society is complicit. It is therefore up to the State to take care of the little hands that would have to suffer from this reconversion. In concrete terms, compensation will have to be paid according to the prejudices suffered. But there is no reason to believe that such a conversion will be difficult. It will be necessary to continue to supply food to the population. It will be necessary to grow, transport, process and market plant-based food. This sector will be able to create many jobs quickly. It has a future. It is the future. This moral revolution will not be so difficult to accomplish as soon as we start thinking about it...

Living with animals

This reflection on the practicalities of abolishing slaughterhouses, fishing and hunting is only the beginning. This abolition does not solve all the questions concerning our relationship with animals. Once the principle of non-cruelty has been accepted, there are still many situations where the steps to follow are not clear at first. For example, what to do with your cat who likes to chase mice or birds? What should you do with rats that take up residence in our cities? Should we intervene so that gazelles are not eaten alive by lions, tigers or cheetahs? And so on. These few questions illustrate well the difficulties of defining the relations that we must maintain with the animals that cohabit with us on earth. In short, once we understand that we must not exploit them and be cruel to them, how can we live with animals?

Often, in the animal protection movement, we hear that animals should be left to live in peace, interfering with them as little as possible. The idea is that they are never more fulfilled than when they live in their natural environment. The relevance of this approach is however questionable. In the wild, i.e. where humans do not interfere, wild animals suffer a lot. Can we really consider that this suffering does not concern us? Imagine that, during a walk in the countryside, you come face to face with a wounded doe, unable to move. Would you kick it to death? Do you leave it to die on the spot? Or do you call the veterinary services to take care of it? Chances are, you'll want to save her. The reason is that, deep down, you feel a moral obligation to help a suffering animal.

Of course, this doe is not in the situation of the gazelles that are being eaten. We cannot help the latter without harming the predators that feed on them. It is not that we should not help them. But it is more delicate to do so if it is at the expense of the latter. It seems that there will always be a huge number of animals to be eaten alive. This is the cruelty of nature. We have to live with it. This should not prevent us from intervening here and there, when we have the means to do so and when our help does not have an undesirable effect. There is thus a whole reflection to be undertaken to know how to mitigate the cruelty of this world. How we are to live with animals is thus an open problem awaiting its thinkers.

One thing is certain: there is no longer any question of deliberately making animals suffer and kill them, just on a whim. It is therefore urgent that intellectuals stop supporting all practices that contribute to this gratuitous cruelty. In particular, it is time for them to call for the abolition of slaughterhouses, hunting and fishing...

ACKNOWLEDGEMENTS

I hesitated to write this book. Perhaps there were better things to do than to draw up a long list of nonsense uttered by French "intellectuals" against vegans. But two reasons prompted me to overcome my reluctance. First, in view of the appalling reality of the slaughterhouses, it seemed urgent to me to denounce the responsibility of these "intellectuals" in this massacre, even if it meant using the form of a pamphlet so that the approach would have more resonance. In this matter, the end justified the form. Then, the reading of criticisms, both scathing and argued, against some of these intellectuals persuaded me that the exercise could be instructive. Reading the deconstruction of an ideology is always invigorating. So I thought that I could possibly do useful work by continuing and completing this work of undermining.

Among the criticisms of carnivorous "intellectuals" that have inspired me and taught me a lot to think about are those written by Yves Bonnardel, David Chauvet, Valéry Giroux, Renan Larue, David Olivier, Estiva Reus, Pierre Sigler and

Enrique Utria. I would therefore like to thank these authors warmly. They are the proof that the title of intellectual can be commendable. Finally, this book would certainly have been less relevant if David Chauvet, Renan Larue and David Olivier had not reviewed a first version of the manuscript. So, I would like to thank them again. It goes without saying that the errors and clumsinesses that I would have left in the text are my sole responsibility. Let me just hope that the carnivores will not use this as a pretext to continue to justify massacres from another time...

Table of Contents

Best sellers Max Milo Editions

Hitler's banker, Jean-François Bouchard

Confessions of a forger, Éric Piedoie Le Tiec

The Koran and the flesh, Ludovic-Mohamed Zahed

Governing by fake news, Jacques Baud

Governing by chaos, Collectif

A political history of food, Paul Ariès

Mad in U.S.A.: The ravages of the "American model", Michel Desmurget

Mondial soccer club geopolitics, Kévin Veyssière

Putin: Game master?, Jacques Braud

Treatise on the three impostors: Moses, Jesus, Muhammad, The Spirit of Spinoza

TV Lobotomy, Michel Desmurget

www.ingramcontent.com/pod-product-compliance
Lightning Source LLC
LaVergne TN
LVHW010559060726
842528LV00013B/3074